FLEE ALSO YOUTHFUL LUSTS

AN EXPOSITION OF 2 TIMOTHY 2:22

About the author
Boon-Sing Poh was born in Malaysia in 1954. Brought up in a pagan background, he was saved by God's grace through faith in Jesus Christ while studying in the United Kingdom. He returned to Malaysia to become a lecturer in a university for six years, founded the first Reformed Baptist Church in the country in 1983, and was imprisoned for his faith from 1987 to 1988 for a period of 325 days. He is the pastor of Damansara Reformed Baptist Church (DRBC) in Kuala Lumpur, a contented husband, a thankful father of four sons, and a happy grandfather. He earned the PhD degree in Electronics Engineering from the University of Liverpool, UK, the Diploma in Religious Study from Cambridge University, UK, and the PhD degree in Theology from North-West University, SA.

FLEE ALSO YOUTHFUL LUSTS

AN EXPOSITION OF 2 TIMOTHY 2:22

BOON-SING POH

PUBLISHED BY
GOOD NEWS ENTERPRISE

FLEE ALSO YOUTHFUL LUSTS: An Exposition Of 2 Timothy 2:22

Copyright ©Boon-Sing Poh, 2019

ISBN: 978-983-9180-29-9

First published: March 2019

Published by:

GOOD NEWS ENTERPRISE, 52 Jalan SS 21/2,
Damansara Utama, 47400 Petaling Jaya, Malaysia.
www.rbcm.net; www.ghmag.net

Printed by:
Kindle Direct Publishing, an Amazon company, United States of America. Typeset by the author using TeXworks, the memoir class.

Dedicated to

all the brethren who have stood with us,

as we strive for greater holiness and usefulness,

in our walk with God.

Contents

FOREWORD

The substance of this book came from a series of talks given during an annual Youth Camp, in which the theme was "Flee Also Youthful Lusts..." (2 Tim. 2:22). As suggested by the theme, the primary purpose is to help the believer handle youthful lusts. The text, namely 2 Timothy 2:22, is expounded so that youthful lusts are identified, dissected, and treated with the biblical remedy.

The verse constituting our text has a complementary part which is stated positively, viz. "but pursue righteousness, faith, love, peace..." This shows that the pursuit of godliness is mandatory, without which the first, and negative, part would be negated or rendered impracticable. The verse ends with the qualification, "...with those who call on the Lord out of a pure heart." This shows that the pursuit of godliness, accompanied by flight from lusts, should be carried out in the context of the local church, and in the company of like-minded believers.

Youthful lusts are not confined to youths, i.e. those who are young in age. They are found in older Christians as well. Older Christians, who have been in the faith for longer, are expected to handle youthful lusts better. However, they must be careful not to drop their guard as the serpent in them is always ready to rear its ugly head. It will be tragic for Christians of mature years to fall into youthful lusts and sin against the Lord. Furthermore, mature Christians should understand the struggles of the youths and be ready to guide them.

The process of sanctification is a lifelong affair. The Holy Spirit in us will ensure our victory. God, who has begun the good work in us, will complete it until the day of Jesus Christ. May the Triune God have all the glory!

B S Poh,
Kuala Lumpur, March 2019.

2 Timothy 2:1-26

1 You therefore, my son, be strong in the grace that is in Christ Jesus. 2 And the things that you have heard from me among many witnesses, commit these to faithful men who will be able to teach others also. 3 You therefore must endure hardship as a good soldier of Jesus Christ. 4 No one engaged in warfare entangles himself with the affairs of this life, that he may please him who enlisted him as a soldier. 5 And also if anyone competes in athletics, he is not crowned unless he competes according to the rules. 6 The hardworking farmer must be first to partake of the crops. 7 Consider what I say, and may the Lord give you understanding in all things.

8 Remember that Jesus Christ, of the seed of David, was raised from the dead according to my gospel, 9 for which I suffer trouble as an evildoer, even to the point of chains; but the word of God is not chained. 10 Therefore I endure all things for the sake of the elect, that they also may obtain the salvation which is in Christ Jesus with eternal glory.

11 This is a faithful saying: For if we died with Him, we shall also live with Him. 12 If we endure, we shall also reign with Him. If we deny Him, He also will deny us. 13 If we are faithless, He remains faithful; He cannot deny Himself.

14 Remind them of these things, charging them before the Lord not to strive about words to no profit, to the ruin of the hearers. 15 Be diligent to present yourself approved to God, a worker who does not need to be ashamed, rightly dividing the word of truth. 16 But shun profane and idle babblings, for they will increase to more ungodliness. 17 And their message will spread like cancer. Hymenaeus and Philetus are of this sort, 18 who have strayed

concerning the truth, saying that the resurrection is already past; and they overthrow the faith of some. 19 Nevertheless the solid foundation of God stands, having this seal: "The Lord knows those who are His," and, "Let everyone who names the name of Christ depart from iniquity."

20 But in a great house there are not only vessels of gold and silver, but also of wood and clay, some for honor and some for dishonor. 21 Therefore if anyone cleanses himself from the latter, he will be a vessel for honor, sanctified and useful for the Master, prepared for every good work. 22 Flee also youthful lusts; but pursue righteousness, faith, love, peace with those who call on the Lord out of a pure heart. 23 But avoid foolish and igno- rant disputes, knowing that they generate strife. 24 And a servant of the Lord must not quarrel but be gentle to all, able to teach, patient, 25 in humil- ity correcting those who are in opposition, if God perhaps will grant them repentance, so that they may know the truth, 26 and that they may come to their senses and escape the snare of the devil, having been taken captive by him to do his will.

One

PLOTTING THE DIRECTION

The theme for this series of articles is "Flee Also Youthful Lusts". It is taken from 2 Timothy 2:22. We wish to consider how to handle youthful lusts in the Christian life. Youthful lusts trouble both youths and those mature in years. The mature believer who has grown in his faith as he walks with God is able to handle temptations better than those younger in years and in Christian experience. However, he is not immune to the temptations of youthful lusts and must still be careful not to be drawn into sin. Our purpose here is to help all believers, and especially youths, to understand the nature of youthful lusts and how to handle them.

We do not want to handle the subject carelessly. We wish to interpret the key verse, 2 Timothy 2:22, correctly to draw out what is actually taught. To do that, we must apply the normal rules of interpreting the Bible. Three important rules of interpreting the Bible are: (i) to understand the words of the text plainly; (ii) to understand the words in context; and (iii) to compare the teaching of the passage with other relevant Scriptures. There are other rules of interpretation which may be regarded as refinements of these three basic rules. For example, we should interpret what is unclear in the light of what is clear, and not *vice versa*. This would be a refinement of the third rule of "comparing Scripture with Scripture". The rules of interpretation are applied to determine the spiritual sense, i.e. what the believer needs to know for his spiritual life. This contrasts with the Roman Catholic view that each passage of Scripture has four layers of meaning – the literal, the moral, the allegorical, and the anagogical. To Roman Catholics, the literal sense is the intended meaning of the scriptural author. The moral sense is the meaning for the conduct of the Christian. The allegorical sense is the New Testament fulfilment of the Old Testament. The anagogical sense shows how all things will ultimately be fulfilled in Christ. For us, the rules of interpretation are to help us determine the one spiritual sense of Scripture. Let us consider what we mean by the three basic rules of interpretation.

In the past, Bible scholars stated the first rule as "taking the words of Scripture literally". The word "literally" was chosen to emphasise the need to avoid wrongful allegorisation. However, it caused many Christians to swing to the other extreme of taking the words of Scripture literalistically. Just as there is a difference between "being simple in faith" and "being simplistic in faith", there is a difference between "understanding the text of Scripture literally" and "understand the text of Scripture literalistically". Those who are literalistic have gone too far to the other extreme from those who wrongly allegorise. To be noted is the fact that some passages of Scripture are clearly figurative and not literal. It would be wrong to take such passages literally. For example, the Lord Jesus Christ says in John 6:51 "I am the living bread which came down from heaven. If anyone eats of this bread, he will live forever; and the bread that I shall give is My flesh, which I shall give for the life of the world." In view of the tendency for many modern Evangelicals to take the words of Scripture literally when the text is clearly figurative, it would be better to state the first rule of interpretation as "taking the words of Scripture plainly". If the text is plainly literal, we take it literally. If it is plainly figurative, we take it figuratively. The rule of "plain sense" covers the intent of what was formerly stated as the rule of "literal sense".

The second rule of interpretation is "to take the words of Scripture in context". When words are taken out of context, anything can be made out of them. It is important, therefore, to read the verses before and after the passage so that we know the context, or circumstances, in which the passage occurs. There is the immediate context to consider, and there is the wider context to consider as well. At the minimum, the immediate context must be taken into account. Often, the wider the context we consider, the better it will be for us to understand the passage correctly.

The third rule of interpretation is to consider a passage of Scripture in the light of other Scriptures that have bearing on the subject. It is not possible for God to contradict Himself by teaching one thing in one passage and a different thing in another passage. If ever we find the teaching in a passage contradicting other passages that speak of the same matter, it is either we have wrongly understood the passage or there is a way of reconciling the apparent contradiction which we have not understood. We must then restudy the subject more carefully until a satisfactory solution is found. The ultimate author of the Bible is God, who inspired chosen men in the past to write down His word by His Spirit. The word of God cannot contradict itself.

Our aim in this first chapter is to plot the direction for this series of studies. For a ship to sail, it must have a direction. For us to travel on a journey, we must determine our route. We will do so by applying the three basic rules of interpretation to our key text. We do not want to begin our journey without first deciding on our destination and the route we wish to take.

1.1 The Meaning

The text
2 Timothy 2:22 says, "Flee also youthful lusts; but pursue righteousness, faith, love, peace with those who call on the Lord out of a pure heart." There are two complementary parts to this verse, both of which are in the imperative sense. In other words, the two parts come to us as commands. The first part says "Flee also youthful lusts..." To flee is to run away from something. It is to keep an increasing distance from something. In this case, we are commanded to run away from youthful lusts. Note that the word "lusts" is in the plural, showing that there are more than one type of lusts. This point is often missed by the casual reader, who would then conclude that this is a reference to one particular type of lust, viz. the sexual ones. The word "lusts" means strong desires, or deep yearnings. Another point to note is that in the original Greek, there is the definite article – it is "*the* youthful lusts" and not merely "youthful lusts". The definite article shows that there were certain lusts well-known to the readers and to Paul, the writer. It indicates that the apostle Paul had been teaching them about these lusts and they were all familiar with his teaching. The "also" (Gk., *de*) is a conjunction often translated as "now" or "but" which does not add material value to the verse. The

5

definite article, however, is significant.

The context
This epistle was written to Timothy, to be read to the church in Ephesus where he was placed as the pastor. The teaching of this verse – and of the whole epistle – was directed to Timothy and all those who heard this epistle read out. Timothy was a young man, estimated to be between 37 and 42 years of age.[1] He was not yet past 60 years old. Being relatively young, he still had to be careful of youthful sins. Older people must not think they are immune to youthful lusts, but this teaching is particularly relevant to youths. Many are the young people in church who struggle with youthful lusts such that their consciences are affected. How they would be helped if correct teaching on this subject is given!

The text occurs in a passage in which Timothy was instructed to train up other teachers of the word. We are told in verse 2, "And the things that you have heard from me among many witnesses, commit these to faithful men who will be able to teach others also." Paul had a four-generation view of gospel ministry. Paul was the first generation, who trained Timothy, the second generation. Timothy was to train up teachers of a third generation who could teach the fourth generation. This was an important task, and constituted a heavy responsibility. There was all the more reason to set a good example for others. Not only was he a pastor who must set a good example for others, he was also to train up other pastors and gospel preachers. The responsibility was great and the need to set a good example is obvious. We therefore read in verses 3 to 7,

> You therefore must endure hardship as a good soldier of Jesus Christ. No one engaged in warfare entangles himself with the affairs of this life, that he may please him who enlisted him as a soldier. And also if anyone competes in athletics, he is not crowned unless he competes according to the rules. The hardworking farmer must be first to partake of the crops. Consider what I say, and may the Lord give you understanding in all things.

Timothy was then reminded of the task of all preachers, viz. the salvation of the elect for whom Christ died. To accomplish the task

[1]Hendriksen, W., 1983. New Testament Commentary: 1 & 2 Thessalonians, 1 & 2 Timothy and Titus. The Banner of Truth Trust.

of calling out the elect from the world, and building them up in the faith, Timothy must endure all things for their sake (verses 8-13). Single-mindedness was needed. While there were times when false teaching must be countered, Timothy must be careful not to be diverted from the work of "rightly dividing the word of truth" (v. 15), i.e. to diligently and correctly teach the truth. Ungodly people would spread wrong teaching, as Hymenaeus and Philetus had been doing, leading many astray (vv. 16-19). This leads to verses 20-21,

> But in a great house there are not only vessels of gold and silver, but also of wood and clay, some for honor and some for dishonor. Therefore if anyone cleanses himself from the latter, he will be a vessel for honor, sanctified and useful for the Master, prepared for every good work.

To be worthy for God's work, we must cleanse ourselves of anything dishonourable. Wooden and clay vessels were used for dishonourable purposes, such as in feeding animals. (This is no disrespect to those who love pets.) We would use the better utensils for ourselves, and reserve the most valuable utensils for use on special occasions, and for special guests. The lesson is clear – we are to be the best that God has made us to be, in order to serve Him. We would need to ask whether we have given of our best to God. This applies to our time, our gifts, and our effort to serve Him. It will not do if we treat the worship of God as of secondary importance, and serve God half-heartedly.

In this context, the words of verse 22 come to us, "Flee also youthful lusts; but pursue righteousness, faith, love, peace with those who call on the Lord out of a pure heart." The chapter ends with a summary of what have been said – avoid foolish and ignorant disputes, be a faithful servant of the Lord in teaching the truth, and in correcting those in error. God will perhaps grant repentance to those who are in error.

Comparing with other Scriptures
What are these youthful desires? The well-known commentator, William Hendriksen, summarises youthful lusts into three categories, viz. *pleasures, power, and possessions.* The reason given for classifying youthful lusts under these three words that begin with the letter "p" is based on the temptation of our Lord in Matthew 4:1-10. The Lord

was tempted in an objective way, that is to say, there were temptations thrown at Him. The Lord was incapable of being tempted subjectively, i.e. to experience temptations within Himself for He was the pure Son of God who is incapable of having sinful thoughts. In Hebrews 4:15, we are told this about the Lord, "For we do not have a High Priest who cannot sympathise with our weaknesses, but was in all points tempted as we are, yet without sin." We can think of at least another passage that lend support to this classification of lusts under the three P's, viz. 1 John 2:16, which says, "For all that is in the world—the lust of the flesh, the lust of the eyes, and the pride of life—is not of the Father but is of the world." The apostle John seems to have the Lord's temptation of Matthew 4 in mind. Let us consider the three categories of youthful lusts.

Firstly, *pleasures* are craving of physical appetites, e.g. the craving for food and drink, for sex, and for beauty and health. The first temptation of the Lord concerns physical appetite. We read in Matthew 4:1-4,

> Then Jesus was led up by the Spirit into the wilderness to be tempted by the devil. And when He had fasted forty days and forty nights, afterward He was hungry. Now when the tempter came to Him, he said, "If You are the Son of God, command that these stones become bread." But He answered and said, "It is written, 'Man shall not live by bread alone, but by every word that proceeds from the mouth of God.' "

Secondly, *power* is the lust to shine, to be dominant, to be number one (to be *numero uno*). This is often seen in those who are young, and rising to the peak of their careers. Not all people crave for power, position, and popularity. Not all crave for influence over others. However, quite a few do. It is seen in women as well as in men. A person who craves for power easily becomes envious of others, and soon become jealous of them. He easily becomes quarrelsome when he does not get what he wants. The second temptation of the Lord concerns power. We read in Matthew 4:5-7,

> Then the devil took Him up into the holy city, set Him on the pinnacle of the temple, and said to Him, "If You are the Son of God, throw Yourself down. For it is written:

'He shall give His angels charge over you,' and, 'In their hands they shall bear you up, lest you dash your foot against a stone.' " Jesus said to him, "It is written again, 'You shall not tempt the Lord your God.' "

Thirdly, the lust for *possessions* consists in the craving for material things and the glory that goes with these. This craving is often found together with the second one, i.e. that of power. However, we may consider them separately. The third temptation of the Lord concerns possessions. We read in Matthew 4:8-10,

Again, the devil took Him up on an exceedingly high mountain, and showed Him all the kingdoms of the world and their glory. And he said to Him, "All these things I will give You if You will fall down and worship me." Then Jesus said to him, "Away with you, Satan! For it is written, 'You shall worship the Lord your God, and Him only you shall serve.' "

The command of our text is that we are to flee from these three basic categories of sinful desires.

1.2 The Complement

Stated positively

The second part of the text is another command which is couched positively, viz. "...but pursue righteousness, faith, love, peace..." This complements the first part, which is stated negatively. We are to flee youthful lusts, but we must also pursue righteousness, faith, love, and peace. While "to flee" is "to run away from", "to pursue" is "to run after". The two actions are to be carried out at the same time. They belong together. They are the two sides of the same coin. The true believer will not only flee from vices, but he will also pursue the virtues. Instead of waiting till we are ill and in need of medicine, why not eat well and be healthy? "Prevention is better than cure." We are to be proactive, and not merely be reactive. It is better to keep ourselves spiritually healthy than to be weak and easily succumb to temptations that come our way. Furthermore, by being kept busy pursuing the things that are good, we will have little time and opportunity to be tempted by various lusts. We have heard of the saying, "The idle mind is the devil's workshop." In the Old Testament, King David was tempted and fell into sin when idle, while his troops were fighting battles (2 Sam. 11:1-5).

We must flee from youthful lusts, but we must also run after spiritual virtues such as righteousness, faith, love and peace. We are reminded of "the fruit of the Spirit" in Galatians 5:22-23, "But the fruit of the Spirit is love, joy, peace, longsuffering, kindness, goodness, faithfulness, gentleness, self-control. Against such there is no law." The list of items is not meant to be exhaustive but are examples of "the fruit of the Spirit". Note that "the fruit" is in the singular, indicating that the list of nine qualities belong together and are inseparable. Those who are led by the Spirit will show all these qualities. Some of these qualities may appear more prominently than others in any individual believer, but they will all be there and they will develop with time. The phrase, "Against such", shows that there are other qualities that have not been listed. e.g. hope, patience, and perseverance. Our text, 2 Timothy 2:22, may be looked at in the same way. The apostle is giving only a sample list of virtues that we must pursue. That being the case, it would facilitate our studies if we can classify them into three categories, to correspond to the three categories of lusts that we must avoid.

Looking at the verse carefully, we realise that the four virtues mentioned can be classified into three categories that involve: (i) our relationship with God; (ii) our character; and (iii) our relationship with others. One way of helping us to see the situation is that we look up to God, we look in at ourselves, and then we look out towards other people. We are to "look up", to "look in", and then to "look out". Briefly speaking, righteousness is behaviour or actions that are in accordance to God's law. A righteous man is one who does what is right in God's sight. Then, faith is confidence and trust in God. It concerns what we are within ourselves – whether we are converted or not. A person who has faith is one who is saved by grace through believing in Jesus Christ. Thirdly, we have love and peace in our relationship with others. Love is doing good to others at an expense to ourselves, because of faith in Jesus Christ. Peace is the absence of ill-feeling towards others. We are at peace with God first, through faith in Jesus Christ who died for us. We are then able to have peace with others. The first great commandment of the Lord is that we love God with all our heart, soul, mind, and strength. The second great commandment is to love our neighbours as ourselves (Mark 12:30,

31).

Comparing with other Scriptures
We have noted that Timothy was to set a good example for others. When compared with the first epistle from the apostle, we find that Timothy was specifically told to set an example for others. We read in 1 Timothy 4:12, "Let no one despise your youth, but be an example to the believers in word, in conduct, in love, in spirit, in faith, in purity." Furthermore, when we compare our text with 1 Timothy 6:11, we find great similarity in the words used, "But you, O man of God, flee these things and pursue righteousness, godliness, faith, love, patience, gentleness." Timothy was to flee the "many foolish and harmful lusts (1 Tim. 6:8)" while pursuing "righteousness, godliness, faith, love, patience, gentleness". The list of virtues to pursue is longer than that in 2 Timothy 2:22, confirming that we were right in seeing the list in our text as an incomplete, and constituting a sample only. The more complete list in 1 Timothy 6:11 can similarly be classified under three categories, viz.:

  i concerning personal behaviour – righteousness;

  ii concerning personal character – godliness (i.e. reverence for God), and faith (i.e. confidence and trust in God);

  iii concerning attitude and behaviour towards others – love, patience, and gentleness.

Again, we are "looking up", "looking in", and "looking out". By looking at the "youthful lusts" under three categories, and the "spiritual virtues" under three categories, we will be able to follow a definite route in our study of how to handle youthful lusts in the Christian life.

1.3   The Qualifying Phrase

The qualifying phrase at the end of our text must be noted, which says, "...with those who call on the Lord out of a pure heart." The pursuit of spiritual virtues cannot be done in isolation. Those who "call on the Lord" are those who have faith in Jesus Christ. In other words, this instruction is directed at believers. It is the same as what is found in Acts 2:21, "...whoever calls on the name of the LORD shall be saved." Spiritual virtues are to be pursued in the company of other believers who share the same desire. We are made social creatures. We cannot run the Christian race alone. We need companionship. While some pride themselves to be loners, the vast majority of us cannot live in isolation from others. We know the well-known story of a piece of burning coal whose fire dies out when taken out of the stove. Coal pieces burn well only when together. Many passages of Scripture may be brought to bear on this truth. An example is Romans 12:1 which says, "I beseech you therefore, brethren, by the mercies of God, that you present your bodies a living sacrifice, holy, acceptable to God, which is your reasonable service." The members of the church are to corporately present their bodies as one living sacrifice to God. Church membership is assumed here. It is expected of every believer to be integrated into the life of a local church.

Another relevant passage is Matthew 28:18-20 – the so-called Great Commission. The Great Commission requires going into the world to make disciples of all the nations. Once disciples are made, they are to be baptised, which has the purpose of incorporating them into the membership of the local church. Baptism has the *meaning* of the person being united to Christ in His death and resurrection. It has the *purpose* of incorporating the person into the local church. The third element of the Great Commission is to teach the new disciples to observe all the Lord's commands. This can be done properly only in the context of the life of the local church.

A third passage that may be considered is 1 Corinthians 12:12, "For as the body is one and has many members, but all the members of that one body, being many, are one body, so also is Christ." In the church, there are members and there are visitors and friends of the church. There are true believers, and there are nominal Christians, i.e. those who are only Christian in name. Even among true believers, there are degrees of commitment to Christ. The situation is similar to a batch of university graduates who all have the same degree in, say, engineering but they are not equally capable as engineers. Some Christians are more committed to Christ than others. Not all Christians are in the same stage of spiritual growth. Some are more mature, while others are new in the faith. Some have been exposed to years of good expository preaching, while others have not had such opportunity. Our text is urging us to keep company with true believers – "...with those who call on the Lord *out of a pure heart*." Common sense will tell us that when we practise a game, say, of badminton with a better player, we will become better at the game. The Bible tells us that "As iron sharpens iron, so a man sharpens the countenance of his friend (Prov. 27:17)."

We must keep company with those who aspire to live well for God.

1.4 The Lessons

True conversion
We have drawn out lessons for ourselves as we proceeded. We must now specifically apply the teaching of 2 Timothy 2:22 to ourselves. The first lesson is that we must be truly converted, i.e. be a true Christian, without which the twin work of "fleeing from youthful lusts" and "running after spiritual virtues" will not be possible. Our text presupposes this. One who is not a true Christian will not have the desire to flee youthful lusts or to pursue righteousness. Indeed, he will not be able to do so. The desire is not in him, and the ability to do what is right is not in him. Both the desire and the ability to do what is right will come to a person only when he repents of his sins and trusts in Jesus Christ alone for salvation. Romans 6:16-18 tells us,

> Do you not know that to whom you present yourselves slaves to obey, you are that one's slaves whom you obey, whether of sin leading to death, or of obedience leading to righteousness? But God be thanked that though you were slaves of sin, yet you obeyed from the heart that form of doctrine to which you were delivered. And having been set free from sin, you became slaves of righteousness.

Without the Holy Spirit dwelling in us, it is impossible to have a genuine desire for holy living, and there will be no ability to obey God. The Holy Spirit dwells in a person when he comes to faith in Jesus Christ. We read in Galatians 3:2, "This only I want to learn from you: Did you receive the Spirit by the works of the law, or by the hearing of faith?" The answer is obvious – we receive the Spirit when we came to faith, upon hearing the gospel. Those who are nominal Christians, i.e. who are only Christians in name, do not have the Spirit in them. "But you are not in the flesh but in the

Spirit, if indeed the Spirit of God dwells in you. Now if anyone does not have the Spirit of Christ, he is not His (Rom. 8:9)."

Integration into the church
The second lesson is that all true believers are expected to be integrated into the life of the local church. We have explained this already. It is in the church that we are strengthened by fellowship with other believers, receive pastoral care, and are mutually edified. We would understand when a believer needs time to know the church before applying for membership with it. Membership with a church is a mutual thing – the church must agree to accept you, and you must desire to be a member. However, we must be careful not to be a visitor for ever. We would miss out on the blessing of church membership.

In exceptional situations, you might choose not to be a member of the church or the church is not ready to accept you, despite your regular attendance there. Exceptions are hard to justify. One will have to have a clear conscience before God over this matter. Granting that such exceptions do exist, it would be good if arrangement is made such that you are as much part of the church as possible. You can talk to the elders of the church about your situation, and pastoral care can be extended to you as a "friend of the church" while you participate in the life of the church as much as possible. In the Jewish synagogues, there were proselytes, i.e. those who worshipped the God of Israel but were not part of the Jewish community (Acts 2:10; 6:5; 13:43). In the case of the Ethiopian eunuch, he was newly converted and was on the way home to Ethiopia (Acts 8:34-40). Circumstances prevented him from becoming a member of a church at that time.

Spiritual growth
The third lesson is that we must grow spiritually. A true Christian cannot remain stagnant in the Christian life. He must grow, or risk falling into temptation and sin. Spiritual growth is constantly urged upon God's children. We are commanded in 2 Peter 3:18, to "grow in the grace and knowledge of our Lord and Savior Jesus Christ." We are told in 1 Peter 2:1,

> Therefore, laying aside all malice, all deceit, hypocrisy, envy, and all evil speaking, as newborn babes, desire the

> pure milk of the word, that you may grow thereby, if indeed you have tasted that the Lord is gracious.

There are members of the church who might not be growing well spiritually. Such individuals are often slack in attendance at meetings and are not well-integrated into the life of the church. They would do the bare minimum to qualify as members and do not have the welfare of the church at heart. This is a phenomenon known in many churches through the centuries. We are told in Hebrews 10:24-25,

> And let us consider one another in order to stir up love and good works, not forsaking the assembling of ourselves together, as is the manner of some, but exhorting one another, and so much the more as you see the Day approaching.

The phrase "as is the manner of some" shows that there were those who were not behaving as they should. Such people are likely to become a problem to the church if they do not put things right quickly. Soon a root of bitterness will develop in them, causing them to backslide spiritually. Church discipline might have to be implemented to restore them. Why wait till problems arise to cause unhappiness to yourselves and to the church? We are to flee youthful lusts, and pursue righteousness, faith, love and peace. We must heed the warning given in Hebrews 12:14-16,

> Pursue peace with all people, and holiness, without which no one will see the Lord: looking carefully lest anyone fall short of the grace of God; lest any root of bitterness springing up cause trouble, and by this many become defiled; lest there be any fornicator or profane person like Esau, who for one morsel of food sold his birthright.

1.5 Summary

The direction for our study on handling youthful lusts has been plotted. We will consider the three categories of youthful lusts that are to be avoided, viz. pleasures, power, and possessions. We will then consider the three categories of spiritual virtues that are to be pursued, viz. righteousness in God's sight, faith within ourselves, and love and peace towards others. There is the proactive aspect of the Christian life as well as the reactive aspect. Both are to be carried out in the company of like-minded Christians.

1 Corinthians 6:12-20

12 All things are lawful for me, but all things are not helpful. All things are lawful for me, but I will not be brought under the power of any. 13 Foods for the stomach and the stomach for foods, but God will destroy both it and them. Now the body is not for sexual immorality but for the Lord, and the Lord for the body. 14 And God both raised up the Lord and will also raise us up by His power.

15 Do you not know that your bodies are members of Christ? Shall I then take the members of Christ and make them members of a harlot? Certainly not! 16 Or do you not know that he who is joined to a harlot is one body with her? For "the two," He says, "shall become one flesh." 17 But he who is joined to the Lord is one spirit with Him.

18 Flee sexual immorality. Every sin that a man does is outside the body, but he who commits sexual immorality sins against his own body. 19 Or do you not know that your body is the temple of the Holy Spirit who is in you, whom you have from God, and you are not your own? 20 For you were bought at a price; therefore glorify God in your body and in your spirit, which are God's.

Two

FLEE THE LUST FOR PLEASURES

The first category of "youthful lusts" is that of pleasure. This concerns our bodily appetites, which may be considered under three sub-categories, viz. the desire for food and drink, the desire for sex, and the desire for beauty and health. The fulfilment of such bodily appetites produces pleasure which is not necessarily wrong since God has joined the pleasure to the appetites. Pleasure, however, is addictive and can gain control over us so that we become slaves to the appetites. All kinds of sinful excess arise out of such bondage.

Here, we consider how Christians should flee from sinful bodily pleasures, focusing on the desire for food and drink, and also on sexual desire. The desire for beauty and health will be considered in the next chapter. Our approach will be to ask the questions – what, when, and how?

2.1   Food And Drink

The right view
We ask first, what is the right view on food and drink? When man was first created, he was allowed to eat all plants. We are told in Genesis 1:29, 'And God said, "See, I have given you every herb that yields seed which is on the face of all the earth, and every tree whose fruit yields seed; to you it shall be for food."' God later imposed upon Adam the condition that he should not eat from the tree of the

knowledge of good and evil, failing which he would die (Gen. 3:16-17). This was a test for Adam, which he failed to keep. Instigated by Satan, Adam and Eve ate of the forbidden tree. Adam and Eve were expelled from the Garden of Eden, to prevent them from eating of the tree of life, which was the symbol of eternal life. Adam and Eve had failed to gain eternal life by works, i.e. by their own effort.

Adam was the representative head of the human race. His fall brought guilt upon himself and the whole human race. If Adam, in his innocency, could not gain eternal life by his own effort, it is impossible for the fallen race of Adam to gain eternal life by works. God revealed to Adam and Eve another way of salvation, namely that which is by grace, through faith in a Saviour who was to come. This was announced in Genesis 3:15 when God said to the serpent, which was actually Satan,

> And I will put enmity between you and the woman, and between your seed and her Seed; He shall bruise your head, and you shall bruise His heel.

This was the first proclamation of the gospel. A Seed of the woman – note, not of Adam, or of Adam and Eve – would come to bruise the head of the serpent while being wounded in the heel. This is a reference to the coming of Jesus Christ, the Son of God, who was conceived by the power of the Holy Spirit and born to Mary but without a human father. By His death on the cross, Jesus Christ was wounded by the serpent. By His resurrection from the dead, Jesus Christ conquered death which is the last stronghold of Satan. The necessity of the death of the Saviour to cover our sin is shown by God slaughtering animals and making tunics of skin for Adam and Eve (Gen. 3:21). Jesus Christ died on the cross as the perfect sacrifice for the sin of His people. John the Baptist was to say of Jesus Christ, "Behold! The Lamb of God who takes away the sin of the world!"

We must come back to consider the right view on food and drink. The human race increased in number, and in iniquity. The depth of depravity the human race sank into can only be imagined, for God found it necessary to destroy everyone except Noah and his household. After the worldwide flood subsided, Noah and his family came our of the ark. One of the first acts he performed was to worship God by offering up clean animals and birds to God as burnt offerings. Noah had taken into the ark seven pairs each of the clean animals, and two pairs each of the unclean animals (Gen. 7:2). God promised never again to destroy every living thing as He had done, i.e. by flood (Gen. 8:20-21). The New Testament shows that God will one day destroy the universe by fire (2 Pet. 3:11-12). Noah and his sons received the mandate first given to Adam and Eve, viz. to be fruitful, to multiply, and to subdue the earth (Gen. 9:1-2 cf. 2:28). It was at this time, after the flood, that God allowed the human race to eat meat. We are told, in Genesis 9:3, "Every moving thing that lives shall be food for you. I have given you all things, even as the green herbs."

When God entered into covenant with the nation of Israel, He imposed upon His people the food laws (Lev. 11). This was to set the nation apart from other nations, to be specially His people. It was also to teach His people the concept of cleanness and uncleanness – in the ceremonial sense. We are told in Leviticus 11:46-47, "This is the law... to distinguish between the unclean and the clean, and between the animal that may be eaten and the animal that may not be eaten." As descendants of Adam and Eve, we have inherited their sinful nature which makes us unclean in the sight of God. We sin against God in thought, words, and deeds. We have a sinful nature, and we lack perfect righteousness to stand before God. We need the blood of Christ, shed on the cross of Calvary, to make us clean. We need the imputed righteousness of Christ to be accepted by God.

With the arrival of Jesus Christ on earth, and by His death on the cross on behalf of His people, the purpose of the ceremonial laws have been fulfilled. The food laws are no longer applicable to God's people. God's people consist of both Jews and Gentiles who have come to faith in Jesus Christ. Those who have faith in Jesus Christ are considered clean before God. The apostle Peter was shown this in a vision in which unclean animals were let down from heaven in a sheet. He was commanded to kill and eat the animals. Peter protested. A voice declared to Peter, "What God has cleansed you must not call common (Acts 10:15)." Not only would the Gentiles be saved through faith in Christ, but the food laws were being abolished as well. The Lord had already taught this in Mark 7:18-19,

> So He said to them, "Are you thus without understanding also? Do you not perceive that whatever enters a man from outside cannot defile him, because it does not enter

his heart but his stomach, and is eliminated, thus purifying all foods?"

It is not required of the Lord's people to keep to the food laws, as is clear from 1 Timothy 4:4, "For every creature of God is good, and nothing is to be refused if it is received with thanksgiving..."

When sinful
Anything right, good and true can be perverted and become wrong. There are two situations in which the consumption of food and drink becomes wrong. The wrong does not lie in the food and drinks, but in the circumstances and manner of consumption. The first instance is in the context of the worshipping of idols, as taught in 1 Corinthians 8:7-13. The idols, in and of themselves, are nothing but the objects they are made from. They do not have power to answer prayers or to cause harm to people. The heathens sin against the true God by paying homage to their man-made gods. When Christians eat food that have been offered to idols, it might cause other Christians to stumble in the faith. Their faith might waver as they wonder why you should be eating such food. Some of them might be embolden to eat as well, resulting in their conscience being hurt since they think such food is unclean. They might also be stumbled thinking that you are participating in the worship of idols. Although the idols are nothing in and of themselves, the worship of idols is linked to the worship of demons. This is taught in 1 Corinthians 10:20-22,

> Rather, that the things which the Gentiles sacrifice they sacrifice to demons and not to God, and I do not want you to have fellowship with demons. You cannot drink the cup of the Lord and the cup of demons; you cannot partake of the Lord's table and of the table of demons. Or do we provoke the Lord to jealousy? Are we stronger than He?

When Matteo Ricci and other Roman Catholic missionaries went to China in the 17th century, they taught their converts that it was alright to burn joss sticks to the ancestors. The converts could participate in the religious ceremonies of the pagans as long as their hearts were not in what they were doing. It is the nature of Roman Catholicism to be syncretistic. Amazingly, there are some Protestant churches today that teach the same thing – claiming that as long as our hearts are not in agreement with what we do, the actions are harmless. To them, offering tea and burning joss sticks at the altar table to the deceased ancestors is permissible to Christians. The Bible, however, teaches the doctrine of separation. For example, in 1 Corinthians 14:14-18 says,

> Do not be unequally yoked together with unbelievers. For what fellowship has righteousness with lawlessness? And what communion has light with darkness? And what accord has Christ with Belial? Or what part has a believer with an unbeliever? And what agreement has the temple of God with idols? For you are the temple of the living God. As God has said: "I will dwell in them and walk among them. I will be their God, and they shall be My people." Therefore "Come out from among them and be separate, says the Lord. Do not touch what is unclean, and I will receive you." "I will be a Father to you, and you shall be My sons and daughters, says the Lord Almighty."

Christians should separate themselves from idol worship. It is a command of God, and we are not to stumble others who are observing us. When converted, I decided to tell my parents nicely that I could no longer take food offered to idols. My mother clicked her tongue and muttered something to the effect that I was harnessed with extra difficulties. She nevertheless set aside a portion of food for me before offering other portions to the idols at home. Making a stand from early will help to make life easier for everyone.

Another situation in which the consumption of food and drinks is sinful is when they are taken to excess. As a general rule, food taken beyond what is needed to remain healthy is sinful. It is legitimate to enjoy eating and drinking, but it becomes sinful when our health is harmed. The Bible does not condemn gluttony directly, but there is indirect teaching against it. In Luke 12:45-46 we read about the unwise steward,

> But if that servant says in his heart, 'My master is delaying his coming,' and begins to beat the male and female servants, and to eat and drink and be drunk, the master of that servant will come on a day when he is not looking for him, and at an hour when he is not aware, and

will cut him in two and appoint him his portion with the unbelievers.

Some Christians are against drinking wine and other alcoholic drinks. The Bible, however, condemns only drunkenness, and not drinking. The Lord turned water into wine at a wedding, showing that wine in itself is not wrong, nor the consumption of wine (John 2:1-12). On the other hand, we are told in 1 Corinthians 6:10 that drunkards are numbered among those who will not inherit the kingdom of God. Wine is used quite widely in cooking, for flavour. We are warned to "abstain from every form of evil" in 1 Thessalonians 5:22. The evil is not in the wine, just as it is not in money. Just as the love of money is a root of all kinds of evil (1 Tim. 6:10), so also the love of drinking. Christians must be careful, therefore, not to cultivate a love for drinking to the extent of "falling into temptation and a snare" (1 Tim. 6:9). Furthermore, we must take into consideration where we drink, and with whom. If drinking alcoholic drinks causes other believers to stumble, why drink? No doubt, the weak should not judge the strong, and hinder their liberty because of their own scruples. However, those who are strong in the faith should heed the teaching of Romans 14:15-17,

> Yet if your brother is grieved because of your food, you are no longer walking in love. Do not destroy with your food the one for whom Christ died. Therefore do not let your good be spoken of as evil; for the kingdom of God is not eating and drinking, but righteousness and peace and joy in the Holy Spirit.

It needs to be pointed out that many families have been destroyed, or made unhappy, because of alcoholic drink. It takes just one member of the family to be addicted to drink to cast the whole family into drawn-out distress. Unlike other food and drinks, excessive alcoholic drink has the effect of numbing the mind and blurring the rational judgement, leading to loss of sobriety. Self-control is governed chiefly by the mind, which regulates the emotion and directs the will. When the chief faculty of the mind is weakened by alcoholic drink, the other faculties will soon collapse. While not advocating teetotalism (i.e. total abstinence from alcohol), the single-minded disciple of Christ would not want to be entangled in the snare of enjoying a drink too many. On special occasions, such as a wedding banquet of non-Christian friends and relatives, wine is often served. One must guard against the likelihood of being pressured by peers to drink, or to drink more. It is for the individual to assess his own strengths and weaknesses, and to live to God's glory.

Fleeing the lust

The final question we seek to answer is, How may we flee from the sinful desire for food and drink? We have noted that eating in excess to the point of harming our health is sinful. Barring unavoidable medical conditions, Christians are a bad testimony to others when they are excessively overweight. We use the word "excessively" because allowance must be made for fluctuations in weight from what is ideal. Furthermore, there are those who are overweight because of medical conditions such as *hypothyroidism* and *Cushing's syndrome*. Hypothyroidism is the condition in which the thyroid gland in the neck does not produce enough of the thyroid hormone, causing fatigue, weight gain, cold intolerance, etc. Cushing's syndrome is caused by the adrenal glands above the kidneys producing too much hormone. The symptoms include easy bruising, weight gain, obesity, and the accumulation of fat in the midsection, the face, and between the shoulders. We sympathise with those who have such medical problems, and would not want them to feel guilty for being overweight. They need to seek medical treatment, while having to struggle with the symptoms.

How may we enjoy food and drinks without going to excess? Before considering obesity we need to understand the phenomenon of being ruled by the pleasure of eating and drinking. One need not be obese while being a slave to eating and/or drinking. We have noted that anything that gives pleasure has the potential of becoming addictive. When enslaved by the pleasure of eating or drinking, we are no longer free. If, in addition to being in bondage to eating and/or drinking one becomes obese or a drunkard, bad testimony to others sets in. Let us be clear of our definition. Each person has an ideal weight for his height, for his age, and for his body type. One can be underweight or overweight at any time. Obesity is the extreme of being overweight. Obesity seems to be a problem of modern living, when quite many people have a sedentary lifestyle. A godly life includes being self-controlled in eating and drinking.

The secret to enjoying food and drink without fearing obesity lies in eating wisely, and not in abstention. Certain types of food must not be eaten too much, and too often. Too much carbohydrates, and too much of protein from meat, are not good for health. As one ages these must be cut down in quantity, and replaced by fruit, vegetables, and water. We cannot escape the formula that governs our body weight:

Energy Input - Energy Output = Fat

Excess food intake of any kind – whether carbohydrates or proteins – will turn into fat in the body. Fatty tissue that forms in the body is difficult to shed. Exercise and the reduction of food intake will only cause the fat globules to shrink, giving the impression that there is reduction in obesity. It takes long-term and persistent effort for the weight loss to be real. Those who are obese or overweight can easily lose weight by eating half the amount of rice (or potatoes, or bread), and eating more vegetables and juicy fruits instead. Food heavy on carbohydrate – such as ice-cream, desserts, and *durian* – may still be eaten, but eaten less.

The connection between our health and our service to God must not be missed. One who is healthy is able to serve the Lord better. The countenance of his face, and his overall demeanour, will be a reflection of his health. Together with his spirituality, a physically fit person is more likely to commend the gospel better than one who is not. Many missionary organisations require that a candidate for the mission field must be physically fit. Our own experience is that a physically fit person is able to negotiate better the jungles of Indonesia, and the mountains of Nepal, during mission trips and while carrying out relief work.

We must aim to be the best that God has made us to be – spiritually, intellectually, and physically. We must give our all to Him in service. "My utmost for His highest" is a good motto for the Christian.

2.2   Sexual Desire

The right view
We again ask the same questions, the first of which is, "What is the right view on sexual desire?" Sexual desire is part of our make-up. God puts sexual desire in us to prepare us for marriage and procre-

ation. Sexual desire begins to operate from puberty onwards – i.e. from round about 10 years of age onwards. Girls tend to develop earlier than boys. Changes begin to occur in our bodies and new emotions begin to appear. Parents must teach about puberty to their children so that they do not become alarmed. Girls will have their first period, when blood flows from their private parts. Boys may have "wet dreams" in which they experience erection in sleep and ejaculate. A strange attraction for the opposite sex begins to appear, turning into "puppy love" for one particular person. This disappears as the person matures, to be replaced by romantic attraction.

Romantic love is a beautiful sensation given by God, albeit spoiled by sin. If the effects of sin can be minimised, the power and beauty of love are enhanced. No measuring device has been invented to measure the strength of love between two individuals. Love has inspired heroic acts, driven individuals to madness, and caused lives to pine away in uselessness. Love stories stir the passion like nothing else. We can think of "Romeo and Juliet", "Dream of the Red Chamber", etc. Love songs decorate many ancient cultures. Love is able to subdue the strongest warrior. It can provoke the greatest jealousy. Love is a many-splendoured thing. For the Christian, a greater love has subdued his all – including romantic love in himself. The love of God in Jesus Christ makes him willing even to forgo romantic love and its demands.

Romantic love is always accompanied by the desire for sexual intercourse, while the desire for sexual intercourse may exist without romantic love. The latter situation is classified as lust. The teaching of the Bible is that sexual intercourse is permissible only in the marriage relationship. When God created Eve out of Adam's rib and brought her to him as wife, sexual relationship was an integral part of their marriage. We are told in Genesis 2:24-25, "Therefore a man shall leave his father and mother and be joined to his wife, and they shall become one flesh. And they were both naked, the man and his wife, and were not ashamed." In Hebrews 13:4 we are told, "Marriage is honorable among all, and the bed undefiled; but fornicators and adulterers God will judge." The sexual urge can be intense, causing one to burn with passion. The apostle Paul says this in 1 Corinthians 7:8-9. "But I say to the unmarried and to the widows: It is good for them if they remain even as I am; but if they cannot exercise self-control, let them marry. For it is better to marry than to burn with passion."

When sinful

When does sexual desire become sinful? We have seen in Hebrews 13:4 that "fornicators and adulterers God will judge". Other Bible passages that condemn adultery and fornication include Matthew 19:8-9 and Revelation 22:15. Adultery is illegitimate sexual intercourse involving a married person. Fornication is any sexual intercourse outside of the marriage relationship, which includes adultery, premarital sex, unnatural sex (oral sex, anal sex), bestiality (i.e. sex with animals), and the like. Bestiality is specifically condemned in Leviticus 18:23 and 20:15-16. Today, some liberal countries are making bestiality no more a crime. Those who love animals would condemn bestiality because it constitutes cruelty to the animals. Our concern is that, morally, it is despicable and condemned in the Bible.

Impurity of mind in connection with sexual desires is also sinful. The Lord says, in Matthew 5:27-28, "You have heard that it was said to those of old, 'You shall not commit adultery.' But I say to you that whoever looks at a woman to lust for her has already committed adultery with her in his heart." God desires inward purity in His people. Sinful actions often arise from prolonged impurity in thoughts. The admiration of beauty, however, is not to be confused with lust. A godly man may see unusual beauty in a woman and give thanks to God for His wonderful gift. There might be some stirring of masculine attraction towards that woman, but that is hardly lust at all. Masturbation disturbs many youths precisely because of the unclean thoughts associated with it. Masturbation is sexual self-stimulation, usually with the hands and/or fingers, until orgasm occurs. Orgasm is the climax of sexual pleasure in which ejaculation, i.e. the discharge of fluid occurs. Both males and females engage in masturbation. Masturbation is often accompanied by sexual fantasising and voyeurism. Sexual fantasising is imagining having sexual relationship with someone. Voyeurism is gaining sexual pleasure by watching others when they are naked or engaged in sexual activity.

Fleeing the lust

How may we flee from sinful sexual desires? We have noted that the Bible prescribes marriage as the only legitimate outlet for sexual desires for those who are unable to exercise self-control. Of course, this is not the chief reason for marriage. Marriage is for companionship and for procreation (Gen. 2:18-20; 1:28). A sexually healthy man finds himself extremely uncomfortable when the semen (male fluid) builds up in his scrotum. If he is able to divert his attention from sexual thoughts – by keeping himself busy in his job, engaging in some hectic sports, or immersing himself in a hobby that he is passionate about – the built-up semen in the scrotum is naturally discharged during urination. The practise of godliness requires us to "make a covenant with our eyes (Job 31:1)", i.e. by an act of the will not to indulge in impure thoughts. In the digital age when the internet and the social media make pornography readily accessible, this becomes all the more important. Pornography has been used as a treatment for those with sexual problems – erectile dysfunction in men, frigidity in women, and homosexuality. The method itself is questionable, and the results have been questionable. Avoiding pornography is an obvious way to flee from sexual lust.

Is masturbation devoid of fantasising and voyeurism sinful? Does it not constitute a legitimate means of releasing sexual pressure in deprived males, and perhaps also in females? Servicemen who are posted overseas, and migrant workers who are away from home for prolonged periods, face tremendous pressure in the sexual realm. During the Second World War, the Japanese army forcefully enlisted native "comfort women" to provide sexual release for their troops as country after country was conquered – a practice for which they are condemned up to today. Modern living requires us to spend the first 25 years of life in studies, from primary to tertiary levels. Some stop schooling earlier, but many young people strive to finish university. Most young people will postpone marriage till they finish studies which means they have to bear up with the sexual desire for longer, until they get married. Is masturbation legitimate for the servicemen, migrant workers, and students? While we are sympathetic to their predicament, we would point to marriage as the biblical means of relieving the problem. It is possible for believers to cultivate spirituality in the company of other believers – a subject we will come to later – and thereby bypass masturbation as a means of sexual release. Together with a regular sports activity or hobby, the sexual urge may be kept under control. As for non-believers, we know that moral reform without regeneration is ineffective. To put it simply, we do not expect non-believers to behave like believers.

In the married life, tension is bound to arise between the couple. They must learn to settle problems as soon as possible, although not necessarily on the same day. We are told in Ephesians 4:26, "'Be angry, and do not sin": do not let the sun go down on your wrath...'

When relationship is strained, the husband should be careful not to seek comfort in another woman's arms. The wife should be careful not to withhold her body from her husband, and thereby using sex as a weapon. Nothing hurts the feeling – and ego – of the man more than to be spurned by his own wife on the marriage bed. Married people must find their satisfaction in their life partners. In Proverbs 5:15-20 the imagery of water is used to portray the joy of faithful marriage, in contrast to infidelity:

> Drink water from your own cistern, and running water from your own well. Should your fountains be dispersed abroad, streams of water in the streets? Let them be only your own, and not for strangers with you. Let your fountain be blessed, and rejoice with the wife of your youth. As a loving deer and a graceful doe, let her breasts satisfy you at all times; and always be enraptured with her love. For why should you, my son, be enraptured by an immoral woman, and be embraced in the arms of a seductress?

A word needs to be said about those who choose not to get married. Three categories of people who remain unmarried are mentioned in Matthew 19:12, "For there are eunuchs who were born thus from their mother's womb, and there are eunuchs who were made eunuchs by men, and there are eunuchs who have made themselves eunuchs for the kingdom of heaven's sake..." The first category are those born sexually handicapped. These would constitute a small number. The second category consists of those deprived of sexual ability by other men, or by accidents. In olden day China, there were the imperial eunuchs who were castrated. The third category consists of believers who choose not to marry in order to devote their lives to God's service. These are godly people gifted with the ability to be self-controlled in their sexual life. Their devotion to the Lord is commended by the apostle Paul in 1 Corinthians 7:32-34,

> But I want you to be without care. He who is unmarried cares for the things of the Lord—how he may please the Lord. But he who is married cares about the things of the world—how he may please his wife. There is a difference between a wife and a virgin. The unmarried woman

cares about the things of the Lord, that she may be holy
both in body and in spirit. But she who is married cares
about the things of the world—how she may please her
husband.

Those who choose not to get married because they have been
unable to find a suitable life-partner belong to this category. God
will give them sufficient grace to cope with their sexuality (2 Cor.
12:9). They will find their temporary sojourn on earth being blessed
by God, while they are made a blessing to many, because they are
"eunuchs for the kingdom of heaven's sake". For the vast majority of
people, marriage should be received as a beautiful gift of God, to be
valued and enjoyed responsibly.

2.3 Summary

Pleasures linked to bodily appetites are given by God. They are to
be accepted with thankfulness and enjoyed appropriately. Pleasures
may become addictive and lead to sins of various kinds. Food and
drink may be enjoyed in moderation, avoiding being associated with
idol worship and causing others to stumble in their faith. Obesity
does not commend the gospel to others, and hinders us from serving
God well. Sexual relationship is legitimate only within the marriage
relationship. It is possible to cultivate purity of mind and life, even
if imperfectly. The individual's body is the temple of the Holy Spirit.
Our bodies are members of Christ. Food and sexual desire are lawful
in their proper places. "All things are lawful for me, but all things are
not helpful. All things are lawful for me, but I will not be brought
under the power of any (1 Cor. 6:12)."

Daniel 4:28-33

28 All this came upon King Nebuchadnezzar. 29 At the end of the twelve months he was walking about the royal palace of Babylon. 30 The king spoke, saying, "Is not this great Babylon, that I have built for a royal dwelling by my mighty power and for the honor of my majesty?"

31 While the word was still in the king's mouth, a voice fell from heaven: "King Nebuchadnezzar, to you it is spoken: the kingdom has departed from you! 32 And they shall drive you from men, and your dwelling shall be with the beasts of the field. They shall make you eat grass like oxen; and seven times shall pass over you, until you know that the Most High rules in the kingdom of men, and gives it to whomever He chooses."

33 That very hour the word was fulfilled concerning Nebuchadnezzar; he was driven from men and ate grass like oxen; his body was wet with the dew of heaven till his hair had grown like eagles' feathers and his nails like birds' claws.

Three

FLEE THE LUST FOR POWER

The lust for pleasure, treated in the previous chapter, is not complete without a consideration of the lust for beauty and health. Although belonging to the category of bodily pleasures, it is also connected with the lust for power. Is it not true that those who lust for power also lust for beauty and health? Did not Qin Shi Huang, the first emperor of China, attempted to find the elixir of eternal life? Did not most ancient emperors surround themselves with bevies of beauties?

Our concern, here, is the lust for power which shows itself on the individual level. It will be seen that pride lies at the bottom of the lust for power. Pride is the mother of many other sins, which brings the downfall of many youths and more mature people. We will continue with the approach of asking "What is the right view?" "When does it become sinful?" and "How do we flee from it?"

3.1   The Lust For Beauty And Health

The right view
What is the right view on beauty and health? We have noted the difference between admiring the beauty of a woman and lusting after the woman. While it is not sinful to admire beauty, we must "make a covenant with our eyes". In other words, we do not keep looking at the person such that it embarrasses her and sinful thoughts begin to creep into us. We must similarly draw a distinction between the sinful pursuit of beauty and the legitimate desire to look good. God created all things "very good" (Gen. 1:31). The goodness was not

only in the quality, but all-round, including physical beauty. The teaching of 1 Peter 3:3-4 is often wrongly taken as against the pursuit of beauty of any kind. The passage says,

> Do not let your adornment be merely outward—arranging the hair, wearing gold, or putting on fine apparel— rather let it be the hidden person of the heart, with the incorruptible beauty of a gentle and quiet spirit, which is very precious in the sight of God.

A comparison is involved between physical adornment and inward spiritual beauty. The latter is better than the earlier, but the earlier is not forbidden or condemned. The ideal is to have both, but with emphasis placed on the latter.

We are told in 1 Corinthians 11:15 that God has given women long hair for her glory, as a covering. Women generally keep their hair to the end of their lives, while men tend to lose hair with age. Today, we know the scientific causes for the difference. Women possess the female hormone – oestrogen – which gives them their dense, long, hair for beauty and to reflect their tenderness of character. Men, on the other hand, have the male hormone – testosterone – which gives them their muscle-bulk and larger bones, while causing male baldness with age. It is not wrong for women to take care of their God-given long hair and to manage it for looks. The principle that applies is that both men and women should look the best that God has made them to be, without failing to pursue godliness in character. "Godliness with contentment is great gain (1 Tim. 6:6)" applies here just as it applies elsewhere. Not everyone is blessed with good looks, which has to do with symmetry and proportion in features. A lady who is below average in physical beauty can still look good by putting on reasonable make-up and wearing moderate adornment. A man who lacks natural good looks can still be pleasant looking when he keeps his hair – or whatever little he has of it – tidy, and dresses neatly.

Attention should be given to how one dresses. Both men and women should be dressed decently and tidily. Why should we allow the Mormons to monopolise the reputation of being well-dressed? Why should Christian ladies be shabbily dressed? And Christian men as well? It does not suit godly men and women to wear clothes that are too scanty, or too tight. Conservative Christian ladies who wear skirts below the knee, and even up to the ankle, have always appeared feminine and appealing. Men who wear well-pressed clothes and trousers are respected by everyone. Wisdom is needed to style the hair as well. A lady with a round face should not have wrapped-around short hair that makes the face appear rounder. Instead, longer hair up to the shoulders, with frills, would be more suitable. A lady with a thin and long-shaped face should not keep long, straight, hair as it will make the face appear even thinner and longer. A stout man should not wear a horizontally striped shirt as it will make him appear broader. A vertically striped shirt would be more appropriate. A thin man should wear a large-checkered shirt while a plump man should wear a shirt that has smaller squares. Similarly, a bigger-sized lady should wear a dress that has small patterns, while a thin lady should wear a dress that has bigger patterns.[2]

Just as adornment of all and any kind has been wrongly frowned upon by many, bodily exercise has been roundly frowned upon by many as well. We are told in 1 Timothy 4:8, "For bodily exercise profits a little, but godliness is profitable for all things, having promise of the life that now is and of that which is to come." Bodily exercise is not condemned here. It is compared with godliness which has lasting value while bodily exercise profits us in bodily health while on earth. In heaven, all our bodies will be transformed to glorified ones and there would be no need for exercise to keep fit. Godliness on earth, on the other hand, will gain for us treasures in heaven. The Lord says, in Matthew 6:19-20, "Do not lay up for yourselves treasures on earth, where moth and rust destroy and where thieves break in and steal; but lay up for yourselves treasures in heaven, where neither moth nor rust destroys and where thieves do not break in and steal." Works of righteousness on earth will be rewarded by the Lord in heaven. We are told in Revelation 22:12, "And behold, I am coming quickly, and My reward is with Me, to give to every one according to his work." Those who merely concern themselves with this life will miss out on eternal life. Those who have eternal life through faith in Jesus Christ will not want to miss out on having good health with which to serve the Lord while on earth. It is a requirement of all credible missionary organisations that candidates for foreign mission fields should have robust health. In our own situation, we find

---

[2]Jones, B. P. 1983. Beauty and the Best. Bob Jones University Press. A helpful book on the subject of biblical femininity in its physical and social manifestations.

those of poor health unable to keep up with our weekly outreach or to join us in the various mission trips. During the relief work following the recent earthquakes in Nepal, our vehicle broke down in the mountains and we had to hike some five hours up and down the mountains. Those with poor health would have been unable to manage that.

When sinful
Physical exercise is good and should be encouraged in an age when most people live sedentary lifestyles and are glued to the computers and the television sets. The ideal is to have bodily exercise as well as godliness, with emphasis placed on the latter. The desire to look good and to be healthy go together. Good looks are maintained by exercise, and exercise will make a person look and feel good. The principle of godliness with contentment applies to both beauty and health (1 Timothy 6:6). Not all of us are blessed with exceptionally good looks and exceptionally good health. However, we must be the best that God has made us to be. The few who are blessed with exceptionally good looks, or good health, must be careful not to become proud or vain. Good looks, especially, when not matched with godliness, is unattractive. Yes, a godly man will not want an ungodly lady, however pretty she may be! The reverse is true as well – no godly lady will want an ungodly man who is good-looking. Good looks attracts attention, but it does not forge lasting relationships.

Sin creeps in when a Christian is discontented with, and resentful of, the looks or health that he has inherited. He questions God and holds unworthy thoughts about God – that He is unfair, that He is cruel and unkind, that He does not care. This tends to happen to those who are not well-grounded in the faith, who have not been conquered by the doctrine of God's grace, who have not understood the depth of their sin and unworthiness before God. Often, Job is quoted as an example of one who was angry at God. The conclusion is then made that it is not wrong for a believer to be angry at God. We contend that it is the wrong understanding of the teaching of Scripture. We should rather conclude that Job's experience shows that it is wrong to be angry at God, or to question His character, words, or actions. Job was rebuked by God (Job 39-41). Job repented of his sin (Job 42). God, in His mercy, restored Job and blessed him. We must trust God and bow to His will when in severe trials. We must be thankful and be content when in the much less severe situation of not having good looks and/or good health. John Calvin and C. H. Spurgeon did not have good health, yet they served the Lord well. Elisabeth Elliot suffered much in her life, yet she remained faithful to God and was useful in His service to the end of her life.

Sinful lust for beauty is seen in those who go for plastic surgery to improve their looks. Cosmetic surgery is still expensive, but those who can afford it should not rush into it without thinking of the biblical principles involved. Apart from the money involved, is it right for us to be discontented with what God has made us to be? Is it right to place ourselves under the unnecessary risk of a botched surgery? The number of cases of botched plastic surgery is surprisingly high, as can be checked up easily on the internet. What is your reaction when you hear that about one in five of those who have plastic surgery are unhappy with the results? That is 20 percent of the people! Assuming that your plastic surgery is successful, can you live with "permanent hypocrisy" in which you have a face that you were not born with? You may change your looks but not your genes. A case in China that was in the news concerned a man who sued his wife for not informing him that she had had plastic surgery before they were married, causing him much distress when their children were not as good looking as their parents. Deception towards the husband was involved, hypocrisy was involved in the wife, and distress was caused to the husband. This is not to condemn all cases of plastic surgery, for we make a distinction between cosmetic surgery and reconstructive surgery, the latter of which is needed in accidents and genetic birth defects.

Sinful lust for health and beauty is seen also in men wanting the muscular, macho, looks and ladies wanting the thin figure. Men would swallow as much as ten eggs per day and take expensive tablets and supplements to build up their muscles. Excessively huge muscles cause the men to look top-heavy, to walk with the typical "ape-like" sway of muscle-builders, and to struggle with obesity when they stop exercise in later years, when their muscles turn to fat. Ladies who have a strong desire to be thin would develop *anorexia* in which there is severe restriction of food intake, or *bulimia* in which food is vomited by physical induction or the use of laxatives. (Vomiting is physically induced by poking the fingers into the back of the throat.) The lust for good looks in such cases in men and ladies has been caused largely by external influences. Such ideas of good looks are not the representative views of the generality of people in the world. Beauty is in the eyes of the beholder. Sensible ladies are not necessarily attracted to muscular men who consume ten eggs per day and walk with their peculiar gait. Sensible men are not necessarily attracted to ladies who put on excessive make-up to cover up their lack of natural beauty.

We are not condemning body builders who take up the sport under controlled regiments. We are not condemning ladies who have to put on more makeup than normal in show businesses. We are defining what constitute sinful lust for beauty and health in Christians.

Fleeing the lust
Men and ladies who take reasonable care of their looks, dress neatly, are polite, and are adorned with true godliness will stand out attractively in the crowd. If that were not the case, how did all the less-than-average looking persons fell in love and were happily married? In the church, we do not want to focus attention only on those who are good-looking. Those who are less well-endowed – including those who are of short stature, plumb, and bald – should be valued as friends as well. Their godliness may outshine those who are better endowed physically. The Lord did not overlook Zacchaeus of short stature (Luke 19:1-8), nor the man who was blind from birth (John 9), bringing salvation to both of them because they were precious in His sight. The sin of lusting for good looks is often found in those who are already quite well-endowed physically, and not with those who are below-average in looks. The same principles should govern our lives regardless of our looks – be the best that God has made you to be, seek first the kingdom of God and His righteousness, be content with what has God has made you to be, and trust Him to provide you with all your needs. A high degree of godliness will be manifested in quiet confidence in the Lord, love for the brotherhood, and a desire to become a blessing to others.

3.2   The Lust For Power And Influence

The right view
The desire for power and influence is normally associated with positions in the government, and in the business world. Since we will be considering the lust for possessions next, we will limit ourselves here to government. The Bible makes it clear that civil authorities are a gift of God to a nation: "...there is no authority except from God, and

the authorities that exist are appointed by God (Rom. 13:1)." They are given the power to punish the wicked and to protect the law-abiding. It is not wrong for a Christian to hold office in government. Biblical examples of godly people who had held high positions in government include Joseph who was prime minister in Egypt, Daniel who was the third ruler in the Babylonian Empire, Esther who was queen in the Medo-Persian Empire, and Mordecai who was second ruler in the Medo-Persian Empire. It is not impossible to hold high positions in government without compromising the faith. Those with the necessary gifts and aptitude may rightly seek for positions of power and influence in government.

When sinful
The desire for positions of power and influence becomes sinful when one is proud or abuses power when in office, or is envious of others in such offices. Nebuchadnezzar was one who became proud of his position. In Daniel 4:30 we read of him boasting, "Is not this great Babylon, that I have built for a royal dwelling by my mighty power and for the honor of my majesty?" That night, God reduced him to one who behaved, and lived, like oxen. When Nebuchadnezzar finally acknowledged God, his reason returned to him and he was restored to his former glory. The officials of the kingdom were an example of envy when they tried to destroy Daniel because of his high office. In Daniel 6:6-9 we read of them plotting for the downfall of Daniel by deceiving King Darius to sign a decree requiring everyone to petition only the king for thirty days, failing which the person would be thrown to the lions. We know the outcome – Daniel was cast into the den of the lions but God sent an angel to shut the lions' mouths.

Our concern is with the ordinary Christian who does not aspire to be in high office. The danger of sinful desire for power may be in them as well. The love for power is shown in individuals who crave for preeminence in whatever company they are in. They may be loud, or they may be quiet, but soon they show themselves to be pushy and wanting their views heard and their opinions accepted. They may hog the limelight in any gathering, but are shunned by others in life because of their attitude of one-upmanship. They desire to be the "number one" – the *numero uno*. This is different from having a healthy ambition, and having the desire to be the best that one can be. When you think too highly of yourself and desire a position of power in your place of work, a sense of rivalry will develop. Envy sets in, which then becomes jealousy. To envy is to wish that you have what others have. To be jealous is to harbour resentment at others for what they have. Envy may lead to jealousy, and jealousy to covetousness. To covet is to desire to have what belongs to another person. Covetousness is sin, as is clear from the Tenth Commandment. Envy and jealousy are sins as well since one who is envious or jealous of others is not content with himself and dissatisfied with what God has given, or not given, him. We have noted what is said in 1 Timothy 6:6, "Now godliness with contentment is great gain." We are told in Romans 12:3, "For I say, through the grace given to me, to everyone who is among you, not to think of himself more highly than he ought to think, but to think soberly, as God has dealt to each one a measure of faith."

The abuse of power is seen not only in those who hold high office but also lower down the scale. It is seen at the place of work, in the home, and also in the church. We consider the church. A pastor holds a position of power. Preaching the word of God wields much power. It influences lives. The abuse of power occurs when the pastor practises "heavy shepherding", i.e. pastoral oversight that encroaches into personal or family life. This is often done by quoting Scriptures to bind the conscience of others. While the opposite, viz. laxity in oversight is to be eschewed, heavy shepherding must not be tolerated. Another way a pastor abuses power is "to lord it over others". He treats church members like his servants. Others are called upon to do work for him and his family which is not connected with the gospel. Such pastors wait to be served and are not willing to serve. Some tasks are regarded as too menial for them. They would not lift a finger to sweep the floor or to wash the dishes. Put that to cultural expectations, or to personal upbringing – it is still unacceptable in the church of Jesus Christ. Such pastors are setting a bad example, and conveying the wrong idea of gospel ministry.

Fleeing the lust
Pride lies at the bottom of the lust for beauty and health, as well as the lust for power and influence. Pride is thinking too highly of ourselves, causing us to despise others. It makes us forget God, and His demands upon us. In practice, what steps may we take to overcome pride and its effects? Here, we may picture the situation as consisting of a dot in the centre, surrounded by two concentric

circles. First, we look at ourselves, then our relationship within the local church, and then our relationship with the wider church of Jesus Christ.

Our concern is the manifestation of the lust for power in the church, which is tied to office in the church. We have noted that this should not be confused with having a healthy ambition to do well, and to be the best that God has made us to be. We may aspire for office in the church but when not appointed, we are not overly disappointed since God is in sovereign control. We take it that it is not the time yet for us to hold office. Those holding positions of responsibility should be careful to avoid "heavy shepherding" and "lording it over others". The office-bearers must beware of these tendencies. The Sunday School teachers and those who are in charge of various departments of gospel work must beware of these as well. The teaching of our Lord, and the example He has set, must be consciously followed. The Lord says, in Mark 10:44-45, "And whoever of you desires to be first shall be slave of all. For even the Son of Man did not come to be served, but to serve, and to give His life a ransom for many." We are told in Philippians 2:5-8,

> Let this mind be in you which was also in Christ Jesus, who, being in the form of God, did not consider it robbery to be equal with God, but made Himself of no reputation, taking the form of a bondservant, and coming in the likeness of men. And being found in appearance as a man, He humbled Himself and became obedient to the point of death, even the death of the cross.

Next to following the Lord's teaching and example, we must practise responsible church membership. The local church is a covenanted community. We are bound to one another voluntarily by oath. While no one is indispensable in the work of God, each one is responsible for the welfare of the church of Jesus Christ. We are told in 1 Corinthians 12:12, "For as the body is one and has many members, but all the members of that one body, being many, are one body, so also is Christ." We are not to think too highly of ourselves and begin to despise others. Equally, we are not to have a false sense of humility and leave the work to others who we claim are better than ourselves. Verse 26 of 1 Corinthians 12 says, "And if one member suffers, all the members suffer with it; or if one member is honored, all the members rejoice with it." Do we practise such responsible church membership?

The third way to counter the lust for power is to love the brotherhood. This is one of the short exhortations given by the apostle Peter in his first epistle. He says, "Honor all people. Love the brotherhood. Fear God. Honor the king (1 Pet. 2:17)." Love for the Lord will be manifested by love for His people. Churches should not engage in carnal rivalry with one another. Pastors should not be undermining one another's ministry. We should rejoice when other churches prosper. Churches of like mind should especially desire for, and work towards, the spiritual prosperity of one another. This does not mean that sin in churches are to be tolerated or that wrong teaching by preachers are to be ignored. These must be corrected and, if necessary, separation invoked. However, we are not to harbour unkind attitudes toward those who are true churches and faithful preachers – who are attempting to live up to the light given them. In the family, are we not grieved when a brother or sister fails, and do we not rejoice when he or she does well? Fraternal love for one another is pleasing to the Lord. In John 17:23 the Lord prayed this for His people – that they "may be made perfect in one, and that the world may know that You have sent Me, and have loved them as You have loved Me." In the fallen world, carnal rivalry between believers, and between churches, is a reality. It must be mortified. The apostle Paul speaks of those who engaged in carnal rivalry in Philippians 2:15-18,

> Some indeed preach Christ even from envy and strife, and some also from goodwill: The former preach Christ from selfish ambition, not sincerely, supposing to add affliction to my chains; but the latter out of love, knowing that I am appointed for the defense of the gospel. What then? Only that in every way, whether in pretense or in truth, Christ is preached; and in this I rejoice, yes, and will rejoice.

3.3 Summary

Although the lust for beauty and health has been classified under bodily pleasure, it is closely related to the lust for power. Underlying the lust for beauty and health, as well as that for power, is pride. Concerning our looks and health, we are to be content with what

God has given us, to be the best of what God has made us to be, and to pursue godliness. The pursuit of godliness is inseparable from the three remedies proposed for the lust for power, viz. to follow the Lord's teaching and example in humility, to practise responsible church membership, and to love the brotherhood. This will keep us away from the envy, jealousy, and covetousness that arise from the lust for power. It will also prevent the abuse of power.

Luke 12:13-34

13 Then one from the crowd said to Him, "Teacher, tell my brother to divide the inheritance with me."

14 But He said to him, "Man, who made Me a judge or an arbitrator over you?" 15 And He said to them, "Take heed and beware of covetousness, for one's life does not consist in the abundance of the things he possesses."

16 Then He spoke a parable to them, saying: "The ground of a certain rich man yielded plentifully. 17 And he thought within himself, saying, 'What shall I do, since I have no room to store my crops?' 18 So he said, 'I will do this: I will pull down my barns and build greater, and there I will store all my crops and my goods. 19 And I will say to my soul, "Soul, you have many goods laid up for many years; take your ease; eat, drink, and be merry." ' 20 But God said to him, 'Fool! This night your soul will be required of you; then whose will those things be which you have provided?'

21 "So is he who lays up treasure for himself, and is not rich toward God."

22 Then He said to His disciples, "Therefore I say to you, do not worry about your life, what you will eat; nor about the body, what you will put on. 23 Life is more than food, and the body is more than clothing. 24 Consider the ravens, for they neither sow nor reap, which have neither storehouse nor barn; and God feeds them. Of how much more value are you than the birds? 25 And which of you by worrying can add one cubit to his stature? 26 If you then are not able to do the least, why are you anxious for the rest? 27 Consider the lilies, how they grow: they neither toil nor spin; and yet I say to you, even Solomon in all his glory was not ar-

rayed like one of these. 28 If then God so clothes the grass, which today is in the field and tomorrow is thrown into the oven, how much more will He clothe you, O you of little faith?

29 "And do not seek what you should eat or what you should drink, nor have an anxious mind. 30 For all these things the nations of the world seek after, and your Father knows that you need these things. 31 But seek the kingdom of God, and all these things shall be added to you.

32 "Do not fear, little flock, for it is your Father's good pleasure to give you the kingdom. 33 Sell what you have and give alms; provide yourselves money bags which do not grow old, a treasure in the heavens that does not fail, where no thief approaches nor moth destroys. 34 For where your treasure is, there your heart will be also."

Four

FLEE THE LUST FOR POSSESSIONS

We have been looking at the three P's – Pleasures, Power, and Possessions. Following the same method as before, we consider the right view on possessions, when it becomes sinful, and how we are to flee from the lust. We may consider this subject under two headings, viz. the desire to be rich and the desire to accumulate property of one kind or another. One concerns the state of being wealthy, the other concerns the possession of physical things. Our purpose, then, is to consider how we should handle the desire to be rich and to accumulate more property.

4.1   The Desire To Be Rich

The right view
We would not draw a distinction between the desire for wealth and the desire to become wealthy. A wealthy person would have wealth in the form of money, jewellery, bonds and shares, companies, businesses, land, and buildings. In biblical times, wealth was measured in the number of animals one had. Abraham and Jacob were notable examples of godly men who were wealthy. Joseph of Arimathea, who requested for the body of the Lord from Pilate, is described as a rich man: "Now when evening had come, there came a rich man from Arimathea, named Joseph, who himself had also become a disciple of Jesus (Matt. 27:57)." These examples show that it is not impos-

sible to be godly while being wealthy. The Lord said this of the rich young ruler, in Luke 18:24,

> How hard it is for those who have riches to enter the kingdom of God! For it is easier for a camel to go through the eye of a needle than for a rich man to enter the kingdom of God.

This is often wrongly understood as teaching the impossibility of rich people becoming true disciples of Jesus Christ. Those who hold to this wrong notion would take the faith of wealthy Christians with suspicion, or they would reason that perhaps these Christians are not quite wealthy yet to disqualify themselves as true disciples of Christ. Those who heard the teaching of the Lord asked the question, "Who then can be saved?" The Lord's answer was, "The things which are impossible with men are possible with God." Rich people are saved by God's grace, just like those who are not rich. Grace overcomes trust in riches, just as it overcomes trust in good works, academic attainment, or birth.

Wealth may be legitimately gained by intelligent hard work, or by inheritance. There are those who work hard but they do not work smart. They might earn a decent living all their lives and never become rich. We have known of those who struggle to earn a living. We have known of others who dream of becoming rich but never quite make it despite their enterprise and failed ventures. Others, however, seem to have the knack to gain riches without resorting to dishonest or illegal means. Wealth gained by hard work and ingenuity, through honest and just means, are to be admired. Others become wealthy by inheritance and are able to invest wisely so that their money produce more money. There have been cases of those who squander away wealth received by inheritance. In our part of the world, there is a common belief that wealth will not last more than three generations in a family. The first generation builds up the wealth, the second generation generates more wealth, and the third generation squanders away all the wealth! This might have been true in some families but it need not be true to all. It is only a warning to the later generations to value the hard work and sacrifices of the earlier generations, and to be wise in conserving the family wealth.

Wealthy people can afford to live comfortably at a level beyond the pale of the ordinary people. That, in itself, is not wrong. In the hearts of many people is the desire to become reasonably wealthy. Who would not want the family to have no worries over money? Money is needed to support the children in their growing years and when they arrive at higher levels of education. Many parents face the struggle of finding the funds needed for their children to go to university. The principle laid down in Scripture is that "the children ought not to lay up for the parents, but the parents for the children (2 Cor. 12:14)."

There will be many who can identify with my experience. There came a time in my life when I applied for a place in some universities overseas. I had wanted so much to become an engineer. When an offer came from one of the universities that I applied for, I went to my mother to announce the good news. My mother stood silent for a moment, then protested, saying, "Where do we have the money for you to study?" I was stunned for a good number of seconds. I had not thought of the funding for my study. I turned away silently to sit in my room to ponder on my situation. The circumstances worked out such that I finally obtained a government scholarship to study overseas. We have a saying that "the blind chicken managed to catch a worm". It appeared as though I got the scholarship by chance. My parents were not well-educated. I had no guidance from anyone knowledgeable in academic matters. I heard of schoolmates applying for places in universities overseas, and followed suit. I saw a scholarship advertised in the newspapers and applied for it. I had been following the advice of a teacher to read the newspapers to improve on my command of language and general knowledge, and spotted the advertisement. On hindsight, we can see the hand of God in all this. There is no such thing as chance. God is always in control.

That was not all. When our four sons grew up and were going for university studies, it was our turn as parents to worry about their funding. The age gaps between the children were just eighteen months apart. The eldest had made it known that from the age of fifteen he had made up his mind to become a doctor. The university course for medicine was expensive and would last a good six years. If the other boys were to go to university one by one, there would be a time when all four were in university! If any one of them were not good at study, or did not want to study, they could find a job and earn an honest living. Since all of them could study and wanted to study, we had to find the money for them. It was a very trying period in our life. After much prayer and some blunders at getting funding, the Lord graciously provided through the soft loan of a friend who turned up unexpectedly. Our boys have finished their university studies. It is now "pay back time" for them. Every month, they send back money to their mum to clear the loan. The aim is to clear the loan as soon as possible.

We are thankful that the Lord provided through this unexpected means. We are not suggesting that this will be the way the Lord provides for you when the time comes. You should be saving up for your children's education from the moment you start working, and perhaps invest your money wisely instead of merely depending on savings in the bank. Legitimate investment is different from engaging in gambling on the stock market. In investment, the money you place in the company is used for its business so that the profit is shared out with all the share-holders. Wisdom and prudence is needed in investment. Having said that, it needs to be remembered that the Lord will provide for His people. We must live within our means and not beyond our means. The pursuit of money is not wrong in itself. Money is needed for our children's education. Money is needed also for gospel work. If God's people do not give regularly, gospel work will be hindered. The Bible has much to say about giving to gospel work (Hag. 1:2-4; 1 Cor. 16:1-2; 1 Tim. 5:17-18). Givings should be made regularly, willingly, privately and according to one's ability (2 Cor. 9:6-11). Money is needed also to support others in need (Acts 20:35). Our aged parents especially should not be forgotten. We are told in 1 Timothy 5:8, "But if anyone does not provide for his own, and especially for those of his household, he has denied the faith and is worse than an unbeliever." Verse 16 of the same chapter says, "If any believing man or woman has widows, let them relieve them, and do not let the church be burdened, that it may relieve those who are really widows."

It is no sin to earn more money, and to desire a comfortable supply of it.

When sinful

While it is no sin to be wealthy, it is hard for a rich person to enter the kingdom of God. The desire to become wealthy, and to keep one's wealth, may become a hindrance to entering the kingdom of God. This was the experience of the rich young ruler of Matthew 19. He had great possessions, which equated with money. He thought he could keep the money while gaining eternal life. His love for money, however, prevented him from following the Lord whole heartedly. It wasn't that the Lord required him literally to get rid of all his possessions. The Lord told him to do so only to expose the fact that his love for his possessions was hindering him from following the Lord sincerely. We have noted that, in the Bible, there had been many rich people who were truly godly – including Abraham, Jacob, and Joseph of Arimathea. It is not a condition of discipleship to get rid of all one's possessions. It is a condition of discipleship to follow the Lord whole heartedly, whether one is rich or poor. The Lord says, in Luke 9:23, "If anyone desires to come after Me, let him deny himself, and take up his cross daily, and follow Me." To deny self is to give up legitimate personal desires when they clash with following the Lord. We are told in 1 Timothy 6:9, "But those who desire to be rich fall into temptation and a snare, and into many foolish and harmful lusts which drown men in destruction and perdition." We must not allow the love of money to rob us of the pursuit of eternal life, through faith in the Lord Jesus Christ.

The love of money can prevent a person from coming to faith in Christ. The love of money can harm people of faith as well. We are told in 1 Timothy 6:10, "For the love of money is a root of all kinds of evil, for which some have strayed from the faith in their greediness, and pierced themselves through with many sorrows." Money itself is not the cause of evil, but the love of money is one common cause of all kinds of evil. It should be noted that the desire to be rich is found not only in those who are already rich but also in those who are not yet rich. Even the poor may be guilty of greed, while the rich may be truly godly. The love of money has harmed relationships, stumbled other believers, and spoilt a good testimony to the world. If not repented of quickly, it causes one to stray from the faith. The rich, in particular, must heed the warnings of 1 Timothy 6:17-19,

> Command those who are rich in this present age not to be haughty, nor to trust in uncertain riches but in the living God, who gives us richly all things to enjoy. Let them do good, that they be rich in good works, ready to give, willing to share, storing up for themselves a good foundation for the time to come, that they may lay hold on eternal life.

There are two problems associated with wealth that must be mentioned. One is the tendency to trust in money to solve all problems. The rich are so used to settling problems in life by using money that their trust tends to be in their money rather than in God. Pious words might be uttered such as, "Let's trust the Lord", or "We will pray about it." However, "the proof of the pudding is in the eating". If the rich person flaunts his wealth, and seems never content with what he has, all his pious words would not mean much to others. Another problem concerns children raised up in wealthy homes. The maid in the house does everything for the growing child – making his bed when he wakes up, carrying his school beg when he goes to school, picking up his socks when he comes home from school, etc. Such a child will grow up spoilt and unable to take care of himself. The time will come when he has to leave home for further education, or for national service. He might have the money to send his clothes to the laundry, but what if there is no laundry in that place? He might have the money to eat out, but what if there is a need to cook his own meal? Those who raise up their children like that are not doing them good. How many are the young people who have had to learn basic living skills and social skills in our church! We have tried not to be too intrusive in our attempt to guide them in these areas, but it gives us a sense of pleasure and privilege to realise that our church is a sort of finishing school for many a young man and many a young lady.

Fleeing the lust

Two things are clear to us – on the one hand, it is needful to earn more money and, on the other hand, there is the danger of lusting for wealth. How may we, as it were, put a wedge between the two so that while we earn more money, we are prevented from being ensnared by the lust for wealth? Scripture provides some pointers which, when followed, will guide us safely along the narrow path of righteous living:

i *We are to work hard to earn a living without being worried about our needs.* The Fourth Commandment requires that we work hard – six days we shall labour, the seventh day we shall rest and keep it holy to God. In Luke 12:22-23, "Therefore I say to you, do not worry about your life, what you will eat; nor about the body, what you will put on. Life is more than food, and the body is more than clothing."

ii *We are to live within our means,* while praying for God to provide for what we need. The Tenth Commandment warns us against covetousness – the desire to have what others have. Contentment with what we have is taught in 1 Timothy 6:6, "Now godliness with contentment is great gain."

iii *We are to seek God and His righteousness,* knowing that the things we need will be provided by God (Luke 12:29-31; Matt. 6:33).

iv *We are to give to needs,* both to the God's work as well as to the needy. "For where your treasure is, there your heart will be also (Luke 12:34)." "It is more blessed to give than to receive (Acts 20:35)."

4.2   The Desire To Accumulate

The right view
We must say something about the desire to accumulate things and property for there are quite many people who, although not having the desire to become wealthy, nevertheless have a strange desire to have more of certain things. Having possessions in relation to wealth is understandable, for a wealthy person is one who has more possessions than an average person. It might be the accumulation of cattle, sheep and goats – as in the days of Abraham and Jacob. Today, it would be the accumulation of properties, viz. houses, shop-lots, condominiums, or land. However, what we are considering now is quite different from the accumulation of things in relation to wealth. Rather, it is the craving to accumulate things of a certain kind, or of all kinds.

The craving to accumulate might have begun as a hobby to collect certain art items, or souvenirs, and even strange objects such as metal springs or preserved insects – which then grew into an obsession to have more. Others collect ordinary objects such as clothes, shoes, hats, or clocks, and the like. We know of a person who collects drift wood, until the items occupy almost the whole house, causing other members of the household to become so frustrated that they have learned to keep silence. We know of another person who collects souvenirs of various kinds, until there is hardly any space left in the house to store more.

A hobby gives one a sense of pleasure. It is a recreation that helps one relax, in a world that is becoming increasingly hectic and complex. Standard hobbies are reading, music, sports, fishing, travel, the collection of stamps and the collection of preserved insects. Some hobbies are more expensive than others. Other hobbies are potentially dangerous, calling into question the ethics of endangering one's life and the lives of others – e.g. sky-diving, bungee jumping, and parkour. We confine ourselves to those that involve collecting items. As in all activities that give pleasure, the danger of getting addicted is there. Self-control, therefore, is called for.

When kept within reason, the desire to collect items is regarded as a hobby. When accumulated to excess, it becomes hoarding. No one would frown upon the pursuit of a hobby. Everyone would begin to sense that things are no longer right when there is hoarding. Hoarding, in essence, is no different from the desire to accumulate wealth. There is lust for more – in the one case it is of things, in the other it is of wealth. The hoarder will be saying in his or her heart, "Is not this great *collection*, that I have built for *a grand display* by my *own ability* and for the honor of my *personal satisfaction*?" Compare these words with Daniel 4:30, "Is not this great *Babylon*, that I have built for *a royal dwelling* by my *mighty power* and for the honor of *my majesty*?"

When sinful

You probably have shuddered at the comparison between the hoarder's sentiment and the words of King Nebuchadnezzar. What has gone wrong? Or when did the hoarder start going wrong? It was when he was not satisfied with what he already had. He has allowed discontent to enter his heart, just like the rich fool in the Lord's parable, in Luke 12:16-20,

> The ground of a certain rich man yielded plentifully. And he thought within himself, saying, 'What shall I do, since I have no room to store my crops?' So he said, 'I will do this: I will pull down my barns and build greater, and there I will store all my crops and my goods. And I will say to my soul, "Soul, you have many goods laid up for many years; take your ease; eat, drink, and be merry." ' But God said to him, 'Fool! This night your soul will be required of you; then whose will those things be which

you have provided?'

Beware of greed! Remember the words of 1 Timothy 5:6, "Now godliness with contentment is great gain." Compare this with the words of verse 5 which says, "...men of corrupt minds and destitute of the truth, who suppose that godliness is a means of gain."

We have described the hoarder who is drawn away by the lust to accumulate more things. There are those who have the tendency of hoarding, although not carried to such extreme. If you are such a person, do be careful not to upset your spouse who might have the opposite tendency of minimalism, i.e. the desire to have few things. In the married life, it is necessary to compromise by not insisting on one's own way. We are not compromising on truth, or principles but on our preferences, for the good of another person. We are showing forth Christ's love to one we love.

Another effect of hoarding is that it causes the house to appear untidy and cramped, which will affect the comfort of all in the family. An untidy house is hardly a home, as the family cannot relax in it. It causes irritability and unhappiness, often without the family knowing the reason why. Coupled with the hoarding of too many things, an untidy house will be a veritable place to avoid. It might be the unwitting reason why the children quarrel with one another so often, and why they prefer to stay out with their friends. Their studies will be adversely affected which, in turn, will cause the parents to be unhappy with them. Related to cluttering and untidiness is the sense of aesthetics – which differ between individuals. Having a good sense of aesthetics is an asset at home, and possibly at work, and in our interaction with others. Personal tastes and culture influence us to some degree. To those of ethnic Chinese descent, red is the auspicious colour. To the Malays, the favourite colour is green, while to the Indians purple is the colour. However, these colours are largely symbolic and for special occasions. In everyday life, some colours are too "loud", while others are too "glum". In the home, there are wall colours that are soothing and homely. Where the children do their studies, the lighting should be sufficiently bright to prevent eyestrain. Lighting that is overly bright, on the other hand, hurts the eyes. Colour-matching for the clothes we wear also affects our interaction with others. We are straying from our immediate topic, but this is mentioned to provide awareness in seemingly unimportant matters that have an effect on our comfort at home.

Hoarding and untidiness is an unnoticed cause of discomfort at home, which affects relationships and the happiness of our children.

Fleeing the lust
We have noted time and again the truth that anything pleasurable is likely to become addictive. The Spirit-filled believer will live a self-controlled life. It is not necessary to "throw the baby out with the bath water". God has given us this world to richly enjoy, with thanksgiving in our hearts. As with the other youthful lusts, the cultivation of personal godliness is essential. We will have more to say about this by and by.

Related to the cultivation of personal godliness is the cultivation of a concern for God's kingdom. When we are actively involved in the extension of God's kingdom, we will be weaned off obsession with the things of this world. He who lays up treasures in this world will not be rich toward God (Luke 12:22). In Luke 12:33-34, the Lord says, "Sell what you have and give alms; provide yourselves money bags which do not grow old, a treasure in the heavens that does not fail, where no thief approaches nor moth destroys. For where your treasure is, there your heart will be also."

4.3   Summary

Our concern is the lust for wealth and the accumulation of property. A rich person can be a godly person. A person who is not rich might lust for wealth or for more of a certain type of possession. We have noted that it is not required of us to literally sell off everything that we have in order to follow the Lord. We are to work hard and to work smart, to gain wealth without lusting to have more. Our focus should be upon being rich towards God. After all, this is a passing world. Our life is so fleeting. We cannot bring the things of this world with us into heaven. Eternal life must be sought more than the things of this world. Jesus Christ is the pearl of great price which we should seek for above all else.

Romans 6:15-23

15 What then? Shall we sin because we are not under law but under grace? Certainly not! 16 Do you not know that to whom you present yourselves slaves to obey, you are that one's slaves whom you obey, whether of sin leading to death, or of obedience leading to righteousness? 17 But God be thanked that though you were slaves of sin, yet you obeyed from the heart that form of doctrine to which you were delivered. 18 And having been set free from sin, you became slaves of righteousness. 19 I speak in human terms because of the weakness of your flesh. For just as you presented your members as slaves of uncleanness, and of lawlessness leading to more lawlessness, so now present your members as slaves of righteousness for holiness.

20 For when you were slaves of sin, you were free in regard to righteousness. 21 What fruit did you have then in the things of which you are now ashamed? For the end of those things is death. 22 But now having been set free from sin, and having become slaves of God, you have your fruit to holiness, and the end, everlasting life. 23 For the wages of sin is death, but the gift of God is eternal life in Christ Jesus our Lord.

Five

THE PURSUIT OF RIGHTEOUSNESS

Our text, which is 2 Timothy 2:22, says, "Flee also youthful lusts; but pursue righteousness, faith, love, peace with those who call on the Lord out of a pure heart." We are not only to do the negative work of fleeing youthful lusts, but also to do the positive work of pursuing righteousness, faith, love, and peace. We have noted that the list of qualities to pursue may be divided into three categories – the first category concerns our relationship with God, which is righteousness; the second concerns our own character, which is faith; and the third concerns our relationship with others, which includes love and peace. We are to "look up to God", to "look in at ourselves", and to "look out to others".

Here, we shall "look up to God", and consider the command to pursue righteousness. What is "righteousness"? Righteousness is basically obedience to God's law. A righteous person is one who keeps God's law, while a godly person is one who attempts to be like God in character. A godly person would be a righteous person, while a righteous person is not necessarily a godly person. The rich young ruler in the Gospels was righteous because he kept God's law, but he was not godly because as he did not have a living relationship with God. Righteousness focuses on the behaviour of the person while godliness focuses on the character of the person. It says in Deuteronomy 6:24-25,

And the Lord commanded us to observe all these statutes,

61

to fear the Lord our God, for our good always, that He might preserve us alive, as it is this day. Then it will be righteousness for us, if we are careful to observe all these commandments before the Lord our God, as He has commanded us.

To fear the Lord our God is to be godly, and to observe all His commandments is to be righteous. The apostle Paul says this of the Jews, in Romans 10:3-5,

> For they being ignorant of God's righteousness, and seeking to establish their own righteousness, have not submitted to the righteousness of God. For Christ is the end of the law for righteousness to everyone who believes. For Moses writes about the righteousness which is of the law, "The man who does those things shall live by them."

The thrust of the passage is that the perfect righteousness needed for salvation does not come from keeping the law of God, but by faith in Jesus Christ. It shows, at the same time, that righteousness is the keeping of the law of God. We are unable to gain perfect righteousness by keeping the law, but Christ has kept the law perfectly on behalf of His people.

Another passage to consider is Luke 1:5-6,

> There was in the days of Herod, the king of Judea, a certain priest named Zacharias, of the division of Abijah. His wife was of the daughters of Aaron, and her name was Elizabeth. And they were both righteous before God, walking in all the commandments and ordinances of the Lord blameless.

What it means to be righteous is defined for us, viz. "walking in all the commandments and ordinances of the Lord".

Having determined what "righteousness" means, we wish to establish three points, viz. (i) we do not have perfect righteousness of our own; (ii) we need the righteousness of God; and (iii) we are expected to live righteously. The basic truth we wish to establish is that those who are saved by the imputed righteousness of Christ must pursue personal righteousness in Christ.

5.1 We Have No Perfect Righteousness

Of the earth

The first point to make is that we have no perfect righteousness of our own in order to be accepted by the holy God. We are of this world. We are descended from Adam and Eve, who were made from the dust of the earth. God made the first man from the dust of the ground and breathed into him the breath of life. This we learn from Genesis 2:7. Eve was made from a rib of Adam. To Adam and Eve was given the mandate, "Be fruitful and multiply; fill the earth and subdue it; have dominion over the fish of the sea, over the birds of the air, and over every living thing that moves on the earth (Gen. 1:28)." Adam was made the representative head of the human race. In the comparison between Christ and Adam, we are told this in Romans 5:15-16,

> But the free gift is not like the offense. For if by the one man's offense many died, much more the grace of God and the gift by the grace of the one Man, Jesus Christ, abounded to many. And the gift is not like that which came through the one who sinned. For the judgment which came from one offense resulted in condemnation, but the free gift which came from many offenses resulted in justification.

The concept of representation is not alien to us. In life, this concept operates in many spheres. The father speaks on behalf of his family in many situations. The headmaster issues statements on behalf of his school. The member of parliament represent the constituents in government. The head of state represents his country in the world. Adam and Eve were warned that on the day they disobeyed God to eat of the forbidden tree, they shall die. They were given so many trees and plants to eat from, except one. Under instigation from Satan, who appeared in the form of the serpent, Eve – followed by Adam – ate of the forbidden tree. Death came to the human race through Adam. Adam's guilt was mankind's guilt. The punishment due to the sin of Adam came to the human race.

Death, in the Bible, means more than the loss of life on earth. It means the immediate breach of fellowship between God and man. It also means that when we die, our souls will plunge into the eternal judgement of hell. The Bible describes hell as the furnace of fire, outer darkness, the place where there will be weeping and gnashing of teeth. The likes of Cain and Judas Iscariot will be there. In Adam, we are guilty before God. We deserve to be in hell. It is pointless protesting that we did not ask to be represented by Adam, just as it is pointless protesting that we did not choose to be born into our particular family.

Without hope
Another problem besets us. Since we are descended from Adam and Eve, we have inherited their sinful nature. The whole human race comes from Adam and Eve. That is why we are so similar to one another, not only in our anatomy but also in our nature. Differences there are – such as the colour of skin, facial features that are sharp or flat, hair that is curly or straight, body to leg proportions that are different, etc. – but these are as nothing compared to the similarities. We all have two eyes, two ears, one nose and out mouth. We do not find any tribe anywhere in the world who have a third eye. Having a third eye occurs only in stories and in paintings. All our facial organs face the front. We do not have ears that are turned backwards, or an eye that is located at the back of the head. The human race was created a class above the animals. There are many "families" among animals. We speak of the cat family which consists of the domestic cat, the wild tiger, the lion, the leopard, and the panther. We have the bovine family that consists of the domestic cow, the buffalo, and the bison. There are also the birds, the reptiles, and the insects. However, there is only one human species. Humans did not evolve from apes. The most intelligent chimpanzee is incapable of inventing tools, learning to count, or engaging in worship like man.

Since we all descended from Adam and Eve, our sinful nature shows itself in common ways. All children grow up showing tantrums, telling lies, and stealing things. As we grow into adulthood, our mind entertains filthy thoughts, our mouth utters lies, and our hands take things that do not belong to us. We sin against God in our thoughts, words and deeds. Our conscience causes us to be uncomfortable – and even miserable – despite our attempts to suppress it. We know that God knows our sins. We instinctively know that we deserve the eternal damnation of hell. We have this twin problems that we cannot solve – we are guilty in the sin of Adam, and we are guilty of the sins we have committed. All the good deeds we try to do cannot make up for our guilt before God. All our effort cannot cleanse our hearts of filth. Physical filth can be cleanse with plentiful water and soap, but not the fifth of the heart.

Left to ourselves we are without hope. We will die in our sin.

5.2 We Need The Righteousness Of Christ

Imputation

Many of us know the story of Martin Luther. He was a monk and theologian in the Roman Catholic Church. He became conscious of his sin before God. He attempted, by his own effort, to make himself better but failed. He engaged in extreme methods of cleansing himself, including climbing up the steps on his knees, but could not gain peace. He read of the "righteousness of God" in the Bible and misunderstood it to mean the righteousness that man produces to meet God's demand. Tried as he did, he could not be assured that he had done enough good works to make up for his sins, nor that his sinful nature was being made clean.

It was while teaching the book of Romans that he discovered the doctrine of "justification by faith". He came to understand that "the righteousness of God" was not the righteousness that man is capable of producing, but the righteousness that God is offering in His Son, Jesus Christ. Jesus Christ claims that He is from heaven and not from the world. The Son of God took for Himself human nature that is free from sin, by being born of the virgin Mary. The Holy Spirit's power operated in Mary, giving her a Son and preventing her sin from passing on to Him. Jesus Christ is that perfect Man who is at the same time the divine Son of God. As God and Man in one person, He laid down His life on the cross of Calvary for the sins of His people. His death paid for the sins of His people, while His resurrection from the dead on the third day gives new life to them. Those who belong to Him – known as the elect, or chosen ones – will repent of sin and trust in Christ for salvation by the hearing of the gospel. When they repent and believe, their sins are regarded as taken away by Christ who died on the cross, while His perfect righteousness is considered given to them. This exchange is what has been called "imputation" – the sins of the believer is imputed to Christ, while Christ's righteousness is imputed to the believer. In that way, the believer is forgiven by God, and accepted by Him as

His child. The believer is declared no more guilty, and treated as righteous. This is justification – the act of being declared no more guilty, and treated as righteous instead.

By grace

Justification is by grace, i.e. by the free gift of God, and not by works done by the sinner. The doctrine of "justification by grace, through faith, in Christ alone" is taught in the Bible. From the beginning, Adam was introduced to the two ways salvation – by works, or by grace. Adam, in his innocency, failed to gain salvation by works. He ate of the forbidden tree, and thus broke God's law. We who are descended from him cannot expect to do any better, as we are now harnessed with a sinful nature inherited from our first parents. Adam was shown another way of salvation which God promised would come through a Seed of the woman. This was a reference to the Lord Jesus Christ. Animals were slaughtered, blood was shed, and the skins used to cover the nakedness of Adam and Eve, showing that Jesus Christ would come to die as "the Lamb of God who takes away the sin of the world (John 1:29)". From the time that Adam fell, no one is able to be saved by works. The religions of the world attempt this way of salvation. All who try to be saved by their own effort – by keeping to rules and rituals, by trying to become righteous – will fail. Jesus Christ is "the way, the truth, and the life". No one can come to the Father except through Him (John 14:6).

While Adam is the head of the human race in respect to the Covenant of Works, Christ is the head of the redeemed race in respect to the Covenant of Grace. The contrast between Adam and Christ is given in Romans 5:18-19,

> Therefore, as through one man's offense judgment came to all men, resulting in condemnation, even so through one Man's righteous act the free gift came to all men, resulting in justification of life. For as by one man's disobedience many were made sinners, so also by one Man's obedience many will be made righteous.

When salvation came to Adam and Eve, by the promise of the Saviour, it did not mean that the whole human race was saved. Rather, the way of salvation, by grace, was revealed to the human race. To obtain salvation, each individual must repent of sins and trust in Christ for eternal life.

In practice, the gospel must be preached to all, to declare the way of salvation in their hearing. The preaching, and hearing, of the gospel is the instrumentality by which salvation comes to sinners. The Holy Spirit will use the gospel that is preached to draw the elect to faith in Christ. We are told in Romans 10:17, "Faith comes by hearing and hearing by the word of God." The gospel must be proclaimed by believers, and it must be heard by unbelievers, for there to be salvation. The apostle Paul summarises the gospel as "Jesus Christ and Him crucified" in 1 Corinthians 2:2. The person and death of Christ must be proclaimed. Christ must be proclaimed as the Son of God, who is the Saviour appointed by God. Christ's death to pay for sins, and His resurrection to give life, is the only way for sinners to be reconciled with God. It is necessary to call upon hearers of the gospel to repent of sins and to trust in Jesus Christ for salvation. Repentance and faith do not add any material value to the salvation which is complete in Christ. Just as the hands that are stretched out to receive a parcel do not add anything to it, so also repentance and faith do not add anything to the gift of salvation. Repentance and faith are the means by which the sinner benefits from the salvation in Jesus Christ.

Salvation is by grace, through faith, in Jesus Christ alone. A double imputation is involved – the imputation of the sin of the believer to Christ in His death, and the imputation of Christ's righteousness to the sinner who believes.

5.3   We Are Expected To Live Righteously

Former slaves of sin
When converted – by grace through faith in Jesus Christ – the person becomes different and will behave differently. Before conversion, sin is the master in his life. He is unable to be free from the power of sin. That is to be expected because he has a sinful nature. The person will behave the way he is – a sinful individual. Left to himself, he will always choose to act contrary to God's law. There may be times when he desires to act in a morally correct way. He may have high morals compared to others but he is unable to do everything right. There will be many, many occasions when he acts in greed, shows his selfishness, or thinks evil of others. Some people are plagued with particular sins. There was the case of a man who could not help

swearing and using filthy words. He tried hard to stop using foul and unkind words, but just couldn't. One day, he used unkind words against his wife. The moment the words came out of him, he realised what had happened. While his wife looked at him, he fell on his bed in exasperation. He just couldn't break away from this terrible habit of his. The story has a happy ending. It was when he committed his life to the Lord that he was delivered from this problem. (For the record, this was not me.)

This condition is a form of slavery. We are slaves of sin, until set free by faith in Christ. When converted, new desires come into our hearts and we are given the ability to obey God. The obedience might not be perfect, but we now begin to willingly do what is right in God's sight. This is taught in Romans 6:17-18,

> But God be thanked that though you were slaves of sin, yet you obeyed from the heart that form of doctrine to which you were delivered. And having been set free from sin, you became slaves of righteousness.

This not only shows that we are set free from the power of sin when we believe in Jesus Christ, but also that we are expected to live a righteous life once we are converted. The process of growing in holiness has been called "sanctification". Sin still remains in us, but it is no longer the master over us. Our worldview has changed. Before conversion, self is at the centre of our lives, while we think of the good of others next, and of obedience to God last, if at all. When converted, the reverse is the case. We now want to obey God above all else, we think of others' good next, and then we think of our own good. This change in our worldview will be seen in our lives. In the first epistle of John the three marks of a Christian are constantly put forward, viz. the doctrinal mark, the moral mark, and the social mark. An example is 1 John 3:4-9, which says,

> Whoever commits sin also commits lawlessness, and sin is lawlessness. And you know that He was manifested to take away our sins, and in Him there is no sin. Whoever abides in Him does not sin. Whoever sins has neither seen Him nor known Him. Little children, let no one deceive you. He who practices righteousness is righteous, just as He is righteous. He who sins is of the devil, for the

devil has sinned from the beginning. For this purpose the Son of God was manifested, that He might destroy the works of the devil. Whoever has been born of God does not sin, for His seed remains in him; and he cannot sin, because he has been born of God.

Present sanctification

Sanctification is the process of growing holier and holier. Holiness is the quality of the person's life while righteousness is the behaviour arising from that quality. A holy person is a godly person, that is to say, he knows God and lives to please Him. A godly person will live a righteous life, thus showing that he is holy. The person's holiness is not perfect, and is growing as the days go by. There will be times when he struggles over temptations and sins. There will be times when he practises self-denial to obey God or for the good of others. Growth in holiness, or sanctification, is a process. It is not an instantaneous event by which one jumps to a higher level of holiness. Beware of teachings that say that you must have a special experience of some kind to arrive at a new level of holiness! Such teachings have come in different dresses, under various names – "entire sanctification", "instantaneous sanctification", "the baptism in the Holy Spirit", etc.

Sanctification is the work of the Holy Spirit in the believer. The Holy Spirit comes to dwell in the person when he trusts in Jesus Christ for salvation. Galatians 3:2-3 says, "This only I want to learn from you: Did you receive the Spirit by the works of the law, or by the hearing of faith?" The answer is obviously, "By the hearing of faith." We are told in Romans 8:9, "But you are not in the flesh but in the Spirit, if indeed the Spirit of God dwells in you. Now if anyone does not have the Spirit of Christ, he is not His." The Holy Spirit in the believer gives him holy desires and the ability to obey God. Furthermore, with sanctification comes assurance of salvation. As the believer grows in holiness, he becomes increasingly assured that he is a true child of God. This is clear from Romans 8:12-17, which says,

> Therefore, brethren, we are debtors—not to the flesh, to live according to the flesh. For if you live according to the flesh you will die; but if by the Spirit you put to death the deeds of the body, you will live. For as many as are led

> by the Spirit of God, these are sons of God. For you did not receive the spirit of bondage again to fear, but you received the Spirit of adoption by whom we cry out, "Abba, Father." The Spirit Himself bears witness with our spirit that we are children of God, and if children, then heirs— heirs of God and joint heirs with Christ, if indeed we suffer with Him, that we may also be glorified together.

Not only will there be increasing assurance of salvation, there also will be the filling of the Holy Spirit, i.e. the mighty working of the Spirit in us, and through us, as we serve the Lord. Those who keep communion with God by feeding on His word and prayer, who trust and obey the Lord, and keep a clear conscience before God and men, may expect to be greatly used by the Lord. These we shall expand upon in the subsequent studies.

5.4 Summary

The command to flee youthful lusts is accompanied by the command to pursue righteousness. This is a reference to righteous living, which begins with a right relationship with God through faith in Jesus Christ. We do not have the perfect righteousness needed to stand before God. God's perfect righteousness is offered to us in Jesus Christ, who died and rose again to save sinners. Our sin is imputed to Christ when He died on the cross, and His righteousness is imputed to us when we repent and believe in Him. All who are truly converted have the Holy Spirit dwelling in them, who gives them holy desires and the ability to obey God. What are some practical implications from all this?

Firstly, the gospel must be proclaimed so that sinners might be set free from sin. That is God's appointed way for the elect to be called out of the life of sin and the world. We would want to continue doing good to all, but lasting good comes only through faith in Jesus Christ.

Secondly, we must preach the full gospel – not a truncated or distorted gospel. The gospel may be summarised as "Jesus Christ and Him crucified". We must not be ashamed to proclaim Christ as the Son of God, who is the only Saviour of sinners. We must not be ashamed to proclaim His death and resurrection, and the need of cleansing by His blood. We must declare the certainty of forgiveness and reconciliation with God upon repentance and belief.

Thirdly, we must strive for greater righteousness in our lives. The desire to trust and obey God is there, but remaining sin and youthful lusts often trouble us. By yielding ourselves to obey the teaching of the Bible, and keeping a clear conscience before God and men, there will be growth in assurance of salvation and the filling of the Holy Spirit for effective service and greater usefulness.

May God help us, and bless us, in our walk with Him.

James 1:1-27

1 James, a bondservant of God and of the Lord Jesus Christ, to the twelve tribes which are scattered abroad: Greetings.

2 My brethren, count it all joy when you fall into various trials, 3 knowing that the testing of your faith produces patience. 4 But let patience have its perfect work, that you may be perfect and complete, lacking nothing. 5 If any of you lacks wisdom, let him ask of God, who gives to all liberally and without reproach, and it will be given to him. 6 But let him ask in faith, with no doubting, for he who doubts is like a wave of the sea driven and tossed by the wind. 7 For let not that man suppose that he will receive anything from the Lord; 8 he is a double-minded man, unstable in all his ways.

9 Let the lowly brother glory in his exaltation, 10 but the rich in his humiliation, because as a flower of the field he will pass away. 11 For no sooner has the sun risen with a burning heat than it withers the grass; its flower falls, and its beautiful appearance perishes. So the rich man also will fade away in his pursuits.

12 Blessed is the man who endures temptation; for when he has been approved, he will receive the crown of life which the Lord has promised to those who love Him. 13 Let no one say when he is tempted, "I am tempted by God"; for God cannot be tempted by evil, nor does He Himself tempt anyone. 14 But each one is tempted when he is drawn away by his own desires and enticed. 15 Then, when desire has conceived, it gives birth to sin; and sin, when it is full-grown, brings forth death.

16 Do not be deceived, my beloved brethren. 17 Every good gift and every perfect gift is from above, and

comes down from the Father of lights, with whom there is no variation or shadow of turning. 18 Of His own will He brought us forth by the word of truth, that we might be a kind of firstfruits of His creatures.

19 So then, my beloved brethren, let every man be swift to hear, slow to speak, slow to wrath; 20 for the wrath of man does not produce the righteousness of God.

21 Therefore lay aside all filthiness and overflow of wickedness, and receive with meekness the implanted word, which is able to save your souls.

22 But be doers of the word, and not hearers only, deceiving yourselves. 23 For if anyone is a hearer of the word and not a doer, he is like a man observing his natural face in a mirror; 24 for he observes himself, goes away, and immediately forgets what kind of man he was. 25 But he who looks into the perfect law of liberty and continues in it, and is not a forgetful hearer but a doer of the work, this one will be blessed in what he does.

26 If anyone among you thinks he is religious, and does not bridle his tongue but deceives his own heart, this one's religion is useless. 27 Pure and undefiled religion before God and the Father is this: to visit orphans and widows in their trouble, and to keep oneself unspotted from the world.

Six

THE PURSUIT OF FAITH AND LOVE

We are to "look up", to "look in", and to "look out". To look up is to consider our relationship with God, in which effort is made to live a righteous life. We do not have the perfect righteousness in ourselves to stand before God. We need the perfect righteousness of God which is found in Jesus Christ. When we repent of our sins and trust in Jesus Christ for salvation, the Holy Spirit comes to dwell in us, giving us holy desires and the ability to obey God. The righteous life must be consciously cultivated.

The next thing is to "look in" at our faith. Righteous living without faith in the Lord will not save because it is not based on the imputed righteousness of Jesus Christ. This was the righteousness of the rich young ruler in the Gospels, as we have seen. No one can come to the Father except through Jesus Christ. We must ensure that the faith we have is genuine, if it is to grow. There is the objective aspect of faith, which concerns definable truths found in the Bible. There is also the subjective aspect of faith, which is experienced in us. Our faith in the Lord may be weak but it will grow, if genuine.

True faith will cause us to "look out" to others for their good. The Lord summarises the Ten Commandments in two, the first of which is, "You shall love the Lord your God with all your heart, with all your soul, with all your mind, and with all your strength", and the second is, "You shall love your neighbor as yourself." Those who love God will love their neighbours. By comparing our text, which is 2 Timothy 2:2, with 1 Timothy 6:11, we have concluded that love includes peace, patience, gentleness, and similar qualities which concern our relationship with others. It is sufficient, therefore, to consider faith and love, to cover the full intent of our text.

Our aim, then, is to show that believers are expected to grow in faith and in love.

6.1   The Pursuit Of Faith

Objective faith

We have noted that objective faith concerns the definable truths of the Bible. It is not mere feelings. Saving faith is based on the doctrine of the Bible that can be articulated and explained. We narrow down our discussion to two matters – the gospel and the object of our faith. God's appointed way for His chosen people to be saved is by the hearing of the gospel. We are told, in Romans 10:17, "Faith comes by hearing, and hearing by the word of God." The essence of the word of God is the gospel, which is the good news of salvation for sinners, provided by God through faith in Jesus Christ. The apostle Paul summarises the gospel as "Jesus Christ and Him crucified" in 1 Corinthians 2:2. The person and the death of Christ constitute the two main elements of the gospel, without which the gospel is incomplete.

Around these two main elements hang the various related elements – such as our sin against God, our guilt before Him, our consequent desert of eternal damnation in hell, and our inability to save ourselves. Other related elements include the necessity of repentance and faith, justification for those who have faith, the imputation of our sin to Christ in His death, the imputation of His righteousness to those who believe, the death of Christ as the perfect substitute, the shedding of His blood for the cleaning of our sins, His resurrection to give eternal life to those who believe, the turning away of God's wrath (also known as propitiation), the forgiveness of sins to those who repent, reconciliation with God to those who are united to Christ by faith. These terms sound rather forbidding, but we have explained them in our earlier studies. Here, our emphasis is that the two main elements of "Jesus Christ and Him crucified" must be kept in mind when proclaiming the gospel. The full gospel does not need be proclaimed in a long message, covering every other related elements. Not all the related elements are explicitly taught in every passage of Scripture but the two main elements should be drawn out each time, for there to be a full gospel.

Then, there is the *object* of faith. All gospel proclamation aims at turning the hearer's attention to Jesus Christ as the object, and His death on the cross as the method, of salvation. Faith in Christ as the Saviour would involve faith in His death to save, and *vice versa*. The gospel is not mere doctrine, but doctrine that draws the hearers to faith in Christ who died and rose again to save sinners. The Lord sets the example of gospel proclamation by constantly turning the attention of His hearers to the necessity of believing in Himself and His death on the cross. An example is found in John 8:21-30,

> Then Jesus said to them again, "I am going away, and you will seek Me, and will die in your sin. Where I go you cannot come." So the Jews said, "Will He kill Himself, because He says, 'Where I go you cannot come'?" And He said to them, "You are from beneath; I am from above. You are of this world; I am not of this world. Therefore I said to you that you will die in your sins; for if you do not believe that I am He, you will die in your sins." Then they said to Him, "Who are You?" And Jesus said to them, "Just what I have been saying to you from the beginning. I have many things to say and to judge concerning you, but He who sent Me is true; and I speak to the world those things which I heard from Him." They did not understand that He spoke to them of the Father. Then Jesus said to them, "When you lift up the Son of Man, then you will know that I am He, and that I do nothing of Myself; but as My Father taught Me, I speak these things. And He who sent Me is with Me. The Father has not left Me alone, for I always do those things that please Him." As He spoke these words, many believed in Him.

Subjective faith

Saving faith has its objective aspect, which means that it is based on the truth of Scripture. Furthermore, it is focused on Jesus Christ, who was crucified, as the object. Doctrine is useful only if it leads us to faith in Jesus Christ. While "Jesus Christ crucified" is the object of faith, that faith in Jesus Christ is subjectively appropriated within the individual. All three faculties of the human personality are involved – the mind, the heart, and the will. The mind is convinced by the truth. The heart is convicted by that truth. The will decides to trust in the Christ revealed in the truth. The effect is that we no longer harbour doubts about Christ, we are fully persuaded that He is the Saviour of sinners, and that He is fully able to save. He who has come from heaven will bring us safely there. His death and resurrection delivers us from the eternal damnation of hell. When so persuaded, the sinner is given the ability by the Holy Spirit to turn away from sin and to trust in Jesus Christ for salvation. Instead of guilt and the fear of damnation, there is now peace with God and assurance of His acceptance. All this comes about by the Holy Spirit using the hearing of the gospel to sow the seed of new life in the hearer. The believer begins to desire the things of God, and to live a holy life. "Whoever has been born of God does not sin, for His seed remains in him; and he cannot sin, because he has been born of God (1 John 3:9)."

The faith in the believer is capable of ebb and flow – i.e. it can be shaken and diminished, or it can be strengthened and increased. The apostles asked the Lord to increase their faith, to which the Lord answered that genuine faith, however small, will grow (Luke 17:5-6). All true disciples of Christ will "grow in the grace and knowledge of our Lord and Savior Jesus Christ (2 Pet. 3:18)." Growth in spiritual maturity is inseparable from growth in the knowledge of our Saviour, i.e. in the teaching of the Bible. The reverse might not be the case, i.e. growth in the knowledge of the Bible does not necessary mean that there will be growth in spiritual maturity. Liberal theologians are full of intellectual knowledge of the Bible, but they do not have saving faith in Christ. Similarly, proud Christians may be full of head knowledge of the Bible, but they have not grown in the grace of the Lord. The Bible urges us to abound in faith (2 Cor. 8:7) and to be strong in faith (Rom. 4:20-24). The first step needed for growth in faith is to value correct teaching and to feed richly upon God's word. Practically, that means attending meetings in church to worship God and to hear His word taught. It is abnormal for a true Christian not to attend church regularly. Hebrews 10:24-25 says, "And let us consider one another in order to stir up love and good works, not forsaking the assembling of ourselves together, as is the manner of some, but exhorting one another, and so much the more as you see the Day approaching."

The hearing of the word of God must be accompanied by obedience to God. James 1:22 says, "But be doers of the word, and not hearers only, deceiving yourselves." Faith will not grow well without obedience to the word, just as the body will not grow well without exercise. A baby who only feeds but does not learn to crawl and to walk will end up unhealthy. We do not want to be the type of believers mentioned in Hebrews 5:12-14,

> For though by this time you ought to be teachers, you need someone to teach you again the first principles of the oracles of God; and you have come to need milk and not solid food. For everyone who partakes only of milk is unskilled in the word of righteousness, for he is a babe. But solid food belongs to those who are of full age, that is, those who by reason of use have their senses exercised to discern both good and evil.

The testing of faith

We move on to an unavoidable aspect of faith, viz. that true faith in Jesus Christ will constantly be tested. In other words, trials of various kinds will come to us so that faith will be exercised. The Lord warns us, in Luke 9:23, "If anyone desires to come after Me, let him deny himself, and take up his cross daily, and follow Me." Self-denial and suffering for the faith are to be expected. We are told in Romans 8:16-17, "The Spirit Himself bears witness with our spirit that we are children of God, and if children, then heirs–heirs of God and joint heirs with Christ, if indeed we suffer with Him, that we may also be glorified together." The apostle also says, in 2 Timothy 3:12, "Yes, and all who desire to live godly in Christ Jesus will suffer persecution."

The first chapter of the epistle of James shows that trials may be from without or from within. James 1:2-3 says, "My brethren, count it all joy when you fall into various trials, knowing that the testing of your faith produces patience." The word for "trials" (Gk. *peirasmos*) is the same as that for "temptation" in verse 12, which says, "Blessed is the man who endures temptation; for when he has been approved, he will receive the crown of life which the Lord has promised to those who love Him." Trouble of various kinds from without will put our faith to the test. Temptation from within will also put our faith to the test. One particular trial must be mentioned, by which we might be stumbled in the faith – namely, the unkind words, the backbiting, and the slander from fellow believers. Remaining sin in believers cause those who are not careful to engage in this particular kind of evil. We are told in James 3:8-10, "But no man can tame the tongue. It is an unruly evil, full of deadly poison. With it we bless our God and Father, and with it we curse men, who have been made in the similitude of God. Out of the same mouth proceed blessing and cursing. My brethren, these things ought not to be so." Even church leaders are capable of this. The apostle Paul tells us, in Philippians 1:15-17, "Some indeed preach Christ even from envy and strife, and some also from goodwill: The former preach Christ from selfish ambition, not sincerely, supposing to add affliction to my chains; but the latter out of love, knowing that I am appointed for the defense of the gospel."

The spiritual dimension of life must not be overlooked. When our faith is tested, Satan and his minions are not far from us. Ephesians 6:12-13 says, "For we do not wrestle against flesh and blood, but against principalities, against powers, against the rulers of the darkness of this age, against spiritual hosts of wickedness in the heavenly places. Therefore take up the whole armor of God, that you may be able to withstand in the evil day, and having done all, to stand." Verse 16 says, "...above all, taking the shield of faith with which you will be able to quench all the fiery darts of the wicked one." Satan is good at shooting fiery darts to cast doubts in us. We must lift up the shield of faith to protect ourselves. We are told in James 4:11, "Do not speak evil of one another, brethren. He who speaks evil of a brother and judges his brother, speaks evil of the law and judges the law. But if you judge the law, you are not a doer of the law but a judge."

We may summarise the types of trial that are experienced in the Christian life – first, there are troubles and persecution from without; second, there are temptations of desires from within; and third, there are the doubts and pain that arise from the unkind and untrue words of other Christians. Satan is behind the trials faced by believers. Keeping in mind the three types of trial will help us to understand how we may strengthen our faith.

We have seen the importance of feeding upon God's word, in a regular manner. We have seen also the importance of obeying God's word. Underneath these two actions is the need to trust God under all circumstances. This is made clear in James 4:7-10 where a series of practical instructions is given, based on trust in God,

> Therefore submit to God. Resist the devil and he will
> flee from you. Draw near to God and He will draw near
> to you. Cleanse your hands, you sinners; and purify
> your hearts, you double-minded. Lament and mourn and
> weep! Let your laughter be turned to mourning and your
> joy to gloom. Humble yourselves in the sight of the Lord,
> and He will lift you up.

We may summarise these under the two well-known injunctions – to trust the Lord and to obey the word of God. We are reminded of the refrain in the well-known hymn "When we walk with the Lord" – viz. "Trust and obey, for there is no other way, to be happy in Jesus but to trust and obey."

Feed on God's word. Trust the Lord. Obey His word.

6.2 The Pursuit Of Love

The nature of Christian love

Christian love, or *agape* (in Greek), must not be confused with the other types of love such as those of romance, between family members, or between friends. Christian love may be defined as doing good to others at the expense of self, arising from the life of God in us. This love is shown supremely in the coming of Jesus Christ to earth as stated in John 3:16, "For God so loved the world that He gave His only begotten Son, that whoever believes in Him should not perish but have everlasting life." Non-Christians may show kindness to others which superficially resembles Christian love but, in reality, they are different in nature. In 1 Corinthians 13:13, love is among the three graces (or spiritual virtues) that continue on, in contrast to the sign gifts such as tongue-speaking and prophecy which would fade away – "And now abide faith, hope, love, these three; but the greatest of these is love." If faith and hope are unique to Christians, so is love. Hebrews 11:1 says, "Now faith is the substance of things hoped for, the evidence of things not seen."

Since faith is tied to hope, we need to say more about the latter. Romans 8:24-25 explains to us what hope is, "For we were saved in this hope, but hope that is seen is not hope; for why does one still hope for what he sees? But if we hope for what we do not see, we eagerly wait for it with perseverance." Our faith in Christ secures for us the certainty of acquittal on judgement day and the certainty of our arrival in heaven. This certainty of the future constitutes Christian hope. It is described as "the full assurance of hope" in Hebrews 6:11. It is compared to an anchor in Hebrews 6:19, "This hope we have as an anchor of the soul, both sure and steadfast, and which enters the Presence behind the veil..." Hope is like an anchor that holds down the ship from drifting away. It produces patience, or perseverance in the faith, in the Christian (Rom. 8:25).

Just as faith is tied to hope, so also both these are tied to love. We are told in 1 Thessalonians 5:8, "But let us who are of the day be sober, putting on the breastplate of faith and love, and as a helmet the hope of salvation." We have seen that 1 Corinthians 13:13 shows love to be the greatest of the three because it continues on in heaven. When we are born again of the Holy Spirit, we are enabled to love God and to love the brotherhood of believers. In fact, love for fellow-believers is a mark of true faith in Jesus Christ. This is shown in such passages as 1 John 3:10-12 and 4:7-11,

> In this the children of God and the children of the devil are manifest: Whoever does not practice righteousness is not of God, nor is he who does not love his brother. For this is the message that you heard from the beginning, that we should love one another, not as Cain who was of the wicked one and murdered his brother. And why did he murder him? Because his works were evil and his brother's righteous.

> Beloved, let us love one another, for love is of God; and everyone who loves is born of God and knows God. He who does not love does not know God, for God is love. In this the love of God was manifested toward us, that God has sent His only begotten Son into the world, that we might live through Him. In this is love, not that we loved God, but that He loved us and sent His Son to be the propitiation for our sins. Beloved, if God so loved us, we also ought to love one another.

Love for the brethren

How does Christian love show itself? It is not a mere feeling, although the feeling is involved. We do care for others – that's why we are concerned for them. It is more accurate to describe it as an inner disposition, i.e. an attitude, which manifests itself in action. It is given to us when we are converted. It is listed with the other spiritual virtues which constitute the fruit of the Spirit. We are told, in Galatians 5:22-26,

> But the fruit of the Spirit is love, joy, peace, longsuffering, kindness, goodness, faithfulness, gentleness, self-control. Against such there is no law. And those who are Christ's have crucified the flesh with its passions and desires. If we live in the Spirit, let us also walk in the Spirit. Let us not become conceited, provoking one another, envying one another.

That is the nature of love. It is accompanied by the other qualities like joy, peace, long-suffering, kindness, goodness, faithfulness, gentleness, and self-control in our interaction with others. Negatively speaking, we would not become conceited, provoking one another, envying one another. Positively speaking, we would think the best of others and endeavour to do them good, even at our own expense. This is stated in 1 Corinthians 13:4-7,

> Love suffers long and is kind; love does not envy; love does not parade itself, is not puffed up; does not behave rudely, does not seek its own, is not provoked, thinks no evil; does not rejoice in iniquity, but rejoices in the truth; bears all things, believes all things, hopes all things, endures all things.

Sadly, love between brethren is often disrupted by remaining sin in us, causing faith to be tested – as we have seen. The unity between believers is disrupted, as a consequence. Thankfully, the disruption of unity between the brethren will not be to the extent of disrupting our witness to the world. That is because the Lord prayed for unity among His disciples, in the high-priestly prayer of John 17:20-23,

> I do not pray for these alone, but also for those who will believe in Me through their word; that they all may be one, as You, Father, are in Me, and I in You; that they also may be one in Us, that the world may believe that You sent Me. And the glory which You gave Me I have given them, that they may be one just as We are one: I

in them, and You in Me; that they may be made perfect in one, and that the world may know that You have sent Me, and have loved them as You have loved Me.

Love shown by the church

We now consider love shown on the corporate level by the church. We have shown elsewhere that the church should have a ministry that is patterned after the ministry of the Lord Jesus Christ.[3,4] After John the Baptist was imprisoned, the Lord launched His public ministry by declaring the theme, in Matthew 4:17, "Repent, for the kingdom of heaven is at hand." This may be called the "Mission Statement" of the Lord. This had been declared by His forerunner, John the Baptist, in Matthew 3:2. The Lord next showed how this was to be carried out. His ministry would consist of the three elements of teaching those who are believers, reaching the non-believers with the gospel, and doing good works in conjunction with teaching and preaching. We are told in Matthew 4:23, "And Jesus went about all Galilee, teaching in their synagogues, preaching the gospel of the kingdom, and healing all kinds of sickness and all kinds of disease among the people." This three-pronged approach was carried out consistently by the Lord, as shown in Matthew 9:35, at the peak of His ministry. The apostle Paul imitated the Lord not only in the carrying out of the Great Commission but also in the way ministry was carried out. In Acts 20, he shows us that the gospel was preached publicly and from houses to house (vv. 20-21), the believers were built up in the faith (v. 27), and good works was quietly carried out (vv. 34-35). We emphasise that the good works was carried out quietly because Paul is known more for his teaching and the defence of the truth than for his good works. This is consistent with the Lord's teaching in Matthew 6:3, "But when you do a charitable deed, do not let your left hand know what your right hand is doing..."

Love for others should be shown in action. We are told, in James 1:22, "But be doers of the word, and not hearers only, deceiving yourselves." We are told further in James 2:17-20,

---

[3]Poh, B. S., 2017. THOROUGHGOING REFORMATION: What It Means To Be Truly Reformed.

[4]Poh, B. S., 2019. WORLD MISSIONS TODAY: A Theological, Exegetical, and Practical Perspective of Missions.

> Thus also faith by itself, if it does not have works, is dead. But someone will say, "You have faith, and I have works." Show me your faith without your works, and I will show you my faith by my works. You believe that there is one God. You do well. Even the demons believe—and tremble! But do you want to know, O foolish man, that faith without works is dead?

Evangelical Christians have struggled over the relative importance of preaching the gospel and doing good works. Some have gone astray by preaching the social gospel, a message of deliverance from social oppression and abject poverty. Others have emphasised doing good works only on the personal level, as a fruit of faith in Jesus Christ. The impression given is that good works is an optional matter. The teaching of Scripture, however, is that good works should be pressed upon believers. We are told in Titus 3:8, "This is a faithful saying, and these things I want you to affirm constantly, that those who have believed in God should be careful to maintain good works. These things are good and profitable to men." We are told further in verse 14, "And let our people also learn to maintain good works, to meet urgent needs, that they may not be unfruitful." In Galatians 6:10, we are told, "Therefore, as we have opportunity, let us do good to all, especially to those who are of the household of faith." Passages like these would point to the need for churches to have a definite programme of doing good works, in which the individual members are to take part in. Just as evangelism is not merely to be left to individual initiative but should be organised by the local church, so also good works. Teaching like this is likely to shock many Reformed people, but we are constraint to teach it because of our conviction that it is biblical. We hasten to add that we are not advocating the preaching of a social gospel but the doing of good works in conjunction with teaching the word of God an preaching the gospel to win souls to Christ. We do not advertise the good works that we do since our burden is to the win souls and to build up the church of Jesus Christ.

When these issues are clear to us, we will have an abundance of opportunity to do good works while preaching the gospel to win souls. We would not neglect the building up of the faith of believers in the church while encouraging and guiding them in local outreach and wider church planting. Our faithfulness in the little will lead to more opportunities to do much.

6.3 Summary

We are to "look in" by ensuring growth in our faith. We are to "look out" by showing love to others. Subjective faith is built upon the objective truth of Scripture, and grows by trusting the Lord under all circumstances, while obeying God's word. Love for God would lead to love for our neighbours in practical ways. The church is to have organised outreach while good works are carried out in conjunction with the preaching and teaching of the word of God. Church members are encouraged to be involved in these, depending on their aptitude and the gifts (or abilities) God has given them.

1 Corinthians 12:12-31

12 For as the body is one and has many members, but all the members of that one body, being many, are one body, so also is Christ. 13 For by one Spirit we were all baptized into one body—whether Jews or Greeks, whether slaves or free—and have all been made to drink into one Spirit. 14 For in fact the body is not one member but many.

15 If the foot should say, "Because I am not a hand, I am not of the body," is it therefore not of the body? 16 And if the ear should say, "Because I am not an eye, I am not of the body," is it therefore not of the body? 17 If the whole body were an eye, where would be the hearing? If the whole were hearing, where would be the smelling? 18 But now God has set the members, each one of them, in the body just as He pleased. 19 And if they were all one member, where would the body be?

20 But now indeed there are many members, yet one body. 21 And the eye cannot say to the hand, "I have no need of you"; nor again the head to the feet, "I have no need of you." 22 No, much rather, those members of the body which seem to be weaker are necessary. 23 And those members of the body which we think to be less honorable, on these we bestow greater honor; and our unpresentable parts have greater modesty, 24 but our presentable parts have no need. But God composed the body, having given greater honor to that part which lacks it, 25 that there should be no schism in the body, but that the members should have the same care for one another. 26 And if one member suffers, all the members suffer with it; or if one member is honored, all the members rejoice with it.

27 Now you are the body of Christ, and members in-

dividually. 28 And God has appointed these in the church: first apostles, second prophets, third teachers, after that miracles, then gifts of healings, helps, administrations, varieties of tongues. 29 Are all apostles? Are all prophets? Are all teachers? Are all workers of miracles? 30 Do all have gifts of healings? Do all speak with tongues? Do all interpret? 31 But earnestly desire the best gifts. And yet I show you a more excellent way.

Seven

THE CORPORATE ASPECT OF FAITH

Our text is 2 Timothy 2:22, "Flee also youthful lusts; but pursue righteousness, faith, love, peace with those who call on the Lord out of a pure heart." We have expounded the first part – "Flee also youthful lusts" – under the three "P's", i.e. Pleasures, Power, and Possessions. This part is stated negatively, viz. we are to flee, or run away from, these three categories of youthful lusts.

We have also expounded on the second part of our text – pursue righteousness, faith, love... This part is stated positively. We are to pursue, or run after, these virtues. One category of these virtues is righteousness which concerns our relationship with God. We are to "look up" to God and seek to live righteously in His sight. We are then to "look in" at ourselves, and ensure growth in our faith – by learning the teaching of Scripture, by trusting the Lord under all circumstances, and by obeying His word. We are also to "look out" to others, and seek to edify them. Love covers all the other qualities connected with our relationship with others, such as peace, long-suffering, kindness, goodness, faithfulness, and gentleness.

The two parts are like the two faces of the same coin. They are inseparable. Both must be carried out. We cannot be fighting a defensive battle all the time – trying to flee from youthful lusts without pursuing righteousness, faith, and love. The two parts together constitute spiritual growth. There is a third part to our text, which is, "with those who call on the Lord out of a pure heart." We have made

89

clear the meaning of this qualifying part of our text. Spiritual virtues are to be pursued in the company of other believers who share the same holy desire. We are social creatures, who need the company of others to live well. Over and above that, we are born again of the Spirit of Christ. We share the same divine life through faith in Christ. It is God's will that His children grow spiritually in the company of other believers in the setting of a local church. This is required by the Great Commission as recorded in Matthew 28:18-20, "All authority has been given to Me in heaven and on earth. Go therefore and make disciples of all the nations, baptizing them in the name of the Father and of the Son and of the Holy Spirit, teaching them to observe all things that I have commanded you; and lo, I am with you always, even to the end of the age." It is urged upon us in Hebrews 10:24-25, "And let us consider one another in order to stir up love and good works, not forsaking the assembling of ourselves together, as is the manner of some, but exhorting one another, and so much the more as you see the Day approaching."

After analysing the three parts, it will be good to see the parts together as a whole. In the language of Mathematics, we may say that after performing "differentiation", we must now do "integration". Looking at the text as a whole, we must note that the two main verbs – "to flee" and "to pursue" – are in the active, present, imperative tense. This means that they are commands to be carried out continuously. The two activities are to be carried out in the company of like-minded people in the church. Our purpose here is to consider in greater detail what is involved as we pursue spiritual growth corporately within the local church. Our focus is on the individual's responsibility in this matter. The "fleeing" and the "pursuing" are acts of the will.

7.1   A Personal Choice

The first thing that can be said about the pursuit of spiritual growth is that it begins as a personal choice. While salvation is by grace, through faith in Jesus Christ, discipleship requires an act of the will. Just as unbelief is an act of the will, so also is faith in Jesus Christ. Unbelievers who know the truth about God and the way of salvation in Jesus Christ but wilfully refuse to repent and believe will be held responsible for their unbelief. This was what happened to the first generation of Israelites who came out of Egypt with Moses. We are told in Hebrews 3:16-19,

> For who, having heard, rebelled? Indeed, was it not all who came out of Egypt, led by Moses? Now with whom was He angry forty years? Was it not with those who sinned, whose corpses fell in the wilderness? And to whom did He swear that they would not enter His rest, but to those who did not obey? So we see that they could not enter in because of unbelief.

The relationship between God's sovereignty in salvation and human responsibility in conversion must be clearly understood. Left to ourselves, we are unable to repent and believe. We are spiritually dead. We are "dead in trespasses and sins (Eph. 2:1)." Spiritual life is compared to natural life. Like Lazarus who died and was without life, we do not have spiritual life in ourselves. When the word of Christ comes to us in the gospel, the Holy Spirit uses it to impart new life so that we are enabled to respond. The gospel calls upon us to repent and believe. If indeed new life has been implanted in us, we will repent and believe. The ability to repent, and to believe, is given to us by the power of the Holy Spirit. Until we repent of our sins and trust in Jesus Christ to be saved, we cannot say we are converted, or are born again of the Holy Spirit. However, when we do repent and believe, all glory goes to God who has granted us repentance and faith. God, in His sovereignty, has incorporated human responsibility to accomplish His will in us. Human responsibility is subsumed under divine sovereignty. Human responsibility is not altered in anyway in its character. Just as all events occur under the providence of God, human responsibility has always been subsumed under divine sovereignty. This way of understanding the relationship between divine sovereignty and human responsibility is better than seeing it as an antinomy, i.e. as two apparently contradictory truths that are held in tension together. There is no tension between the two. God is truly sovereign over all events in the whole of creation, including what humans decide to do. Humans are given the freedom to choose, without external coercion. Despite that, all their decisions are such that God's will is fulfilled.

The point we are making is that God does hold us responsible for our actions. We must heed the teaching of the Bible "to grow in the grace and knowledge of our Lord and Saviour, Jesus Christ (2 Pet. 3:18)." Similarly, we are told by the Lord in Luke 9:23, "If anyone desires to come after Me, let him deny himself, and take up his cross daily, and follow Me." To be true disciples of Christ, we must decide to follow Him – accepting all the accompanying self-denial, sacrifices, and sufferings that come to us daily on account of faith. Those who are not prepared to do so will not be able to live the life of true faith in Christ. We have seen how the rich young ruler turned away sadly because he was unable to do what was required of him by the Lord. In the Sermon on the Mount, the Lord tells us "Enter by the narrow gate; for wide is the gate and broad is the way that leads to destruction, and there are many who go in by it. Because narrow is the gate and difficult is the way which leads to life, and there are few who find it. (Matt. 7:13-14)." The life of faith begins with a deliberate choice on our part, which we are enabled to make by God's grace.

The journey of faith requires that we enter it by the narrow gate, which is faith in Christ alone, who died on the cross to save sinners. There is no possibility of carrying anything with us as we squeeze through that narrow gate. Not only must the life of habitual sin be left behind, so must any attempt to bring in human merits. The Lord would not want us to claim we have entered the kingdom of God because we have prayed much, or we have fasted often, or we have done much good works. No human effort can contribute to our salvation. All other ways of salvation are like the wide gate and the broad way that leads to destruction. The Jews attempted to gain salvation by their effort of keeping God's law. The religions of the world teach the need for human merits of some kind or other to gain salvation. The Lord Jesus Christ declares, in John 14:6, "I am the way, the truth, and the life. No one comes to the Father except through Me." There is a tendency today for people to be tolerant of others in the wrong way. To be tolerant over differences in food, lifestyle, politics, etc. does not mean we are not allowed to proclaim the exclusive claims of the gospel. We have the right to teach what we believe, to anyone who is willing to listen, without imposing our views on others. Others are free to teach what they believe for as long as they do not impose their views on us. We must uncompromisingly proclaim that to be saved, one must make the decision to reject reliance on human effort and, instead, embrace salvation by grace, through faith in Jesus Christ.

True faith does not come by self-effort. It also does not come by birth from believing parents or into a Christian community. True faith is not imposed upon us by law or by pressure from the community. Instead, it is given to those who have heard the gospel, who are convinced of the truth in Christ, who are convicted of their guilt before God, and who are converted because of the work of the Holy Spirit in them. In conversion, the Holy Spirit uses the gospel that is heard to convince, convict, and convert. "Faith comes by hearing, and hearing by the word of God (Rom. 10:17)." When the mind is convinced, and the heart is convicted, the will acts in repentance and faith to show true conversion.

7.2   Separation From The World

The second thing that can be said is that the pursuit of spiritual growth requires separation from the world, i.e. from worldliness and unbelief. We are unable to separate ourselves from the world physically. It is not required of us to remove ourselves from the world when we are converted. We are "the salt of the earth" and "the light of the world" (Matt. 5:13, 14). For salt to perform its functions of flavouring the world and preventing it from decaying too fast, we need to interact with it. If the light of the gospel is to benefit others, we need to be in the world. We are "in the world but not of the world". While in the world, we are to guard ourselves from being influenced by it values. This is where we are commanded to flee youthful lusts – of pleasures, power, and possessions. The manifestation of these external expressions of youthful lusts must be traced to the internal values of worldliness that have entered into us. The attempts to stop the pursuit of pleasures, power, and possessions will not succeed if the root of inner desires for these things is not cut.

It is clear that what we believe affects how we behave. When our text, which is 2 Timothy 2:22, is considered in context, we see the necessity of separation from false teaching and false teachers. False teaching is described as "profane and idle babblings" which lead to ungodliness. Hymenaeus and Philetus were purveyors of falsehood who had strayed concerning the truth. Verse 19 of the chapter says, 'Nevertheless the solid foundation of God stands, having this seal: "The Lord knows those who are His," and, "Let everyone who names the name of Christ depart from iniquity."' The true church of Jesus

Christ is made up of those who are known, or loved, by the Lord. They are characterised by holiness of life. We are not saying they are perfect – with no sin ever committed, and with no flaw in all that they do. Rather, we are saying that they are habitually living a righteous life. Perfection will be seen in them only when they are in heaven. While on earth, those who are true Christians will be making effort to live in obedience to God's word. This requires departing from iniquity, i.e. avoiding sinful actions. Sins such as adultery, stealing and lying, which are forbidden in the Ten Commandments, are taken lightly by the people of the world. While it is impossible to withdraw from interacting with non-believing people in the world, we must not be influenced by them. Strong words are used in James 4:4 concerning this matter, "Adulterers and adulteresses! Do you not know that friendship with the world is enmity with God? Whoever therefore wants to be a friend of the world makes himself an enemy of God." Similar teaching is given in 2 Corinthians 6:14-18, with the call given in verse 17, "Come out from among them and be separate, says the Lord. Do not touch what is unclean, and I will receive you."

False teaching leads to ungodliness. We are to separate from false teaching and shun ungodliness. We are also to avoid false teachers. These include the teachers of other religions and the cults. Cults are religious movements that call themselves Christian but are seriously wrong on fundamentals of the faith – such as on the doctrine of God, of salvation, or of the Christian life. We would regard the Jehovah's Witnesses and the Mormons (or Church of the Latter Day Saints) as cults. There are also lesser known cults such as the Eastern Lightning in China. While such false teachers must be avoided, in the sense that we do not accept their teaching and would never allow them to teach in the church, we must be careful not to abuse their persons or hurl insults at them in daily life. They are fellow humans created in God's image, who have rights as citizens of the country. However, we must be warned against those who are recognised teachers in churches but are purveyors of wrong teachings that are more subtle. Their wrong teachings may be couched in biblical words, or mixed with much that is correct, which makes them all the more dangerous. We are specially to watch out against teachings that undermine the authority of Scripture, the doctrine of God, the gospel, or the necessity of godly living. We must also be careful about teachings that encourage worldliness in living and irreverence in speech and worship. The command to separate from false teachers is clearly taught in the Bible. Some relevant passages include the following:

> Romans 16:17-18, "Now I urge you, brethren, note those who cause divisions and offenses, contrary to the doctrine which you learned, and avoid them. For those who are such do not serve our Lord Jesus Christ, but their own belly, and by smooth words and flattering speech deceive the hearts of the simple."

> 2 John 9-11, "Whoever transgresses and does not abide in the doctrine of Christ does not have God. He who abides in the doctrine of Christ has both the Father and the Son. If anyone comes to you and does not bring this doctrine, do not receive him into your house nor greet him; for he who greets him shares in his evil deeds."

We have considered the need to separate from the world, from false teaching, and from false teachers. We must also separate from professing believers who are worldly. Often, the leadership of the church would have instituted discipline against such. As members of the church, we must abide by these disciplinary measures. Furthermore, as a church, we must uphold the disciplinary measures imposed upon an erring member of another church who comes to us. It is possible that the person has been wrongly, or too severely, disciplined. That will take time and interaction between the leadership of both churches to sort out. However, as a general rule, we should uphold the discipline imposed by a true church upon its erring members. Such a person may come to join us in worship, but he may not be allowed to partake of the Lord's Supper or hold any position of responsibility in our church, until he repents and has made up for the wrong with his previous church. The necessity of separation from professing believers who are not walking according to the Bible's teaching is taught in 2 Thessalonians 3:6, 14-15,

> "But we command you, brethren, in the name of our Lord Jesus Christ, that you withdraw from every brother who walks disorderly and not according to the tradition which he received from us...And if anyone does not obey our word in this epistle, note that person and do not keep

company with him, that he may be ashamed. Yet do not count him as an enemy, but admonish him as a brother."

7.3   Separation From Nominalism

Our third point is the need to separate from nominal Christianity. Walking on this earth are many who profess to be Christians when the marks of a true Christian are not seen in them. They do not pray, or live to glorify God, or bear witness for Christ. They do not attend church regularly, or live a righteous life, or know the teaching of Scripture. They are "nominal Christians", i.e. Christians in name only. How does this situation arise? A community or nation could have heard the gospel from missionaries resulting in many being converted. A revival could have occurred in which the vast majority of the people were soundly converted. The first generation of believers could have passed on the gospel to their children, resulting in many being converted as well. However, their faith is not as clearcut as that of their parents, and spiritual decline sets in. The subsequent generations see further spiritual decline, to the extent that now there are many who profess to be Christians but who do not show signs of spiritual life. Nominalism has set in. Many western countries consist of a large proportion of nominal Christians. The church as a whole, and the whole denomination, can become nominal. True Christians, including those converted in such situations, might have to consider leaving for a better church.

On the individual level, nominal Christianity is propagated by the preaching of a distorted gospel or the use of a misleading method of evangelism. In recent years, the altar call is rampantly practised in many churches. In personal evangelism, the "Four Spiritual Laws" of the Campus Crusade For Christ is widely used to extract a profession of faith by reciting the so-called "sinner's prayer". The Charismatic movement has influenced many churches such that those who are induced to "speak in tongues" are pronounced as converted. While it is possible for genuine conversion to take place despite the hearing of a distorted gospel, or the use of a misleading approach in evangelism, there are many who sincerely think they are converted when they are not. They are nominal Christians. When exposed to the true gospel, they either are searched and shaken to the core of their being, or they will become defensive and resentful. By the mercy of

God, a number of such have been soundly converted from nominal Christianity.

True faith in Christ is distinctly different from nominalism. We are told in 2 Timothy 2:20-21,

> "But in a great house there are not only vessels of gold and silver, but also of wood and clay, some for honor and some for dishonor. Therefore if anyone cleanses himself from the latter, he will be a vessel for honor, sanctified and useful for the Master, prepared for every good work."

This is a call to separate ourselves from anyone who teaches error and lives in sin. Associating with such is corrupting, especially if they are leaders in the church. This is also a call to distinguish between true Christianity and nominal Christianity. The pursuit of spiritual growth requires separation from nominal Christianity. We may have nominal Christians in our family, church, or circle of friends. While we have to interact with nominal Christians on the social level, we should not be harnessed to them in the pursuit of righteousness. They do not have spiritual life in themselves. So, how are they to understand what is true righteousness, let alone the pursuit of it? This is where we are not to be "unequally yoked together with unbelievers (2 Cor. 6:14)". We would be respectful to them as fellow humans and sincerely desire their spiritual good, which is different from treating them as God's children and our brethren in Christ. Keeping close company with such may result in our being influenced by them unwittingly. 'Do not be deceived: "Evil company corrupts good habits (1 Cor. 15:33)." '

The pursuit of spiritual growth requires separation from nominal Christianity.

7.4 Commitment To The Local Church

Our fourth point is commitment to the local church. The assumption made in our text is that those addressed are members of a church – "Flee also youthful lusts; but pursue righteousness, faith, love, peace with those who call on the Lord out of a pure heart (2 Tim. 2:22)." The Great Commission of Matthew 28:18-20 is a command to the local church to plant local churches. When disciples are made by the hearing of the gospel, they are to be incorporated into the church by baptism, and taught to obey all the Lord's commands. The local church is made up of baptised believers who are covenanted together to observe all the Lord's commands. The covenant of the church arises from the Covenant of Grace, in which God binds Himself to His people who are called out of the world through the hearing of the gospel. This is taught in Hebrews 8:10-13,

> For this is the covenant that I will make with the house of Israel after those days, says the Lord: I will put My laws in their mind and write them on their hearts; and I will be their God, and they shall be My people. None of them shall teach his neighbor, and none his brother, saying, 'Know the Lord,' for all shall know Me, from the least of them to the greatest of them. For I will be merciful to their unrighteousness, and their sins and their lawless deeds I will remember no more. In that He says, "A new covenant," He has made the first obsolete. Now what is becoming obsolete and growing old is ready to vanish away.

Various illustrations are used to bring home the point that the local church is a community of believers bound together by covenant. We consider only two illustrations here. In 1 Corinthians 12 to 14, the picture of the human body is used. This must be linked to the teaching of Ephesians 5 where Christ is the head while the church is the body. While the word "church" in Ephesians 5 is a reference to the universal body of Christ, it must be kept in mind that the universal church manifests itself in the world as local congregations. The church in Ephesus was a local congregation. The church in Corinth was also a local congregation. The body, which is the church, is made up of many members. There is diversity of gifts in the membership, and there is unity of the members in the body of Christ. "And if one member suffers, all the members suffer with it; or if one member is honored, all the members rejoice with it (1 Cor. 12:26)."

Another illustration is that of the temple of God. We are told, in 1 Peter 2:4-5, "Coming to Him as to a living stone, rejected indeed by men, but chosen by God and precious, you also, as living stones, are being built up a spiritual house, a holy priesthood, to offer up spiritual sacrifices acceptable to God through Jesus Christ." We are living stones, built upon the foundation, who is the Lord Jesus Christ. We are, at the same time, priests in the temple, serving God. Every stone must be in place and fused to the other stones. It wouldn't do to have a stone in place but not fused to the others, let alone being out of place. All these illustrations – the body with many members, the temple made up of living stones, an army, a family, a flock of sheep, a city, etc. – show the necessity of believers being well-integrated in the church, without which the church will not function well and the individuals who are not integrated will not grow well.

This is not to say that at any one moment, the church is totally made up of integrated members. A church – or more accurately, a congregation – will be made up of members and non-members. In 1 Corinthians 14:23-24, we read of those who are "uninformed" and those who are "unbelievers". The "uninformed" are distinguished from the "unbelievers", showing that they are believers but are not members of the church. There will always be visiting Christians who are not members of the church, and unbelievers who are in the church to learn more of the Christian faith. There will be some believers who have been baptised in other churches and are not ready to become members of our church for some reasons. They need time to get to know the church before committing themselves to the membership. We give due allowance for such cases. We would attempt to minister to such as best we can for as long as they are with us. On their part, they should try to be as much part of the church as they are able, and as is allowed by the church.

Commitment to the Lord requires commitment to His church.

7.5 Avoiding Negative Influences

Our fifth point is considered from the position of the individual as a member of a local church – the pursuit of spiritual growth requires that we are not influenced by bad examples from within the church. The membership of the church is not always in the ideal situation of being "of one heart and one soul (Acts 4:32)". In Hebrews 10:24-25, we are urged not to be influenced by the bad example of those who absent themselves from the fellowship of the church. Another relevant passage is 1 Corinthians 3:11-13, "For no other foundation can anyone lay than that which is laid, which is Jesus Christ. Now if anyone builds on this foundation with gold, silver, precious stones, wood, hay, straw, each one's work will become clear; for the Day will declare it, because it will be revealed by fire; and the fire will test each one's work, of what sort it is." Here, the focus is on the quality of service performed by all who belong to the Lord. Although there are degrees in the quality of service, there are those who give of their best to the Lord such that their service may be compared to gold, silver, and precious stones. On the other hand, there are others who give poor quality service to the Lord such that it is like wood, hay, or straw that gets burned away on judgement day. Believers are in mind, for all of them are saved even though some have their works destroyed by the fire of judgement.

In the process of judging our works, there might be those who are found to be merely professing believers who are not born again. In other words, they are not true believers. In the Parable of the Talents in Matthew 25, the one-talent man buried his talent in the ground and returned it to the master, saying, "Lord, I knew you to be a hard man, reaping where you have not sown, and gathering where you have not scattered seed. And I was afraid, and went and hid your talent in the ground. Look, there you have what is yours." The worker is condemned as "wicked" and cast into outer darkness where there will be "weeping and gnashing of teeth". In other words, he is cast into hell. The lesson is clear. Not all who profess to be Christians are true believers. We are reminded of the teaching in Matthew 7:21-23,

> Not everyone who says to Me, 'Lord, Lord,' shall enter the kingdom of heaven, but he who does the will of My Father in heaven. Many will say to Me in that day, 'Lord, Lord, have we not prophesied in Your name, cast out demons in Your name, and done many wonders in Your name?' And then I will declare to them, 'I never knew you; depart from Me, you who practice lawlessness!'

This passage is not a parable. It is a prophecy. On the last day, there will be many – not just a few – who call out "Lord, Lord", and claim that they have served the Lord in various ways, but are disowned by the Lord. We shudder at the fate of such!

We are to keep away from those who set a bad example in the church. In due time, their true spiritual state will manifest itself in some sin, if they do not repent. When that happens, the leadership of the church will have to begin disciplinary procedures against them.

We do not wish to end this section negatively. The reverse is taught in Scripture. While "Evil company corrupts good habits (1 Cor. 15:33)", we learn also that "As iron sharpens iron, so a man sharpens the countenance of his friend (Prov. 27:17)." When we keep company with those who are like-minded in the pursuit of godliness, we derive great encouragement from one another. We are also able to progress well in spiritual things. Knowledge can be taught, but spirituality is largely "caught" rather than "taught".

7.6   Edifying The Church

The sixth point is that the pursuit of spiritual growth should take into account the edification of the local church. The note of edification is strong in the New Testament. We read in 1 Corinthians 10:23, "All things are lawful for me, but not all things are helpful; all things are lawful for me, but not all things edify." In 1 Corinthians 14:26, we have, "How is it then, brethren? Whenever you come together, each of you has a psalm, has a teaching, has a tongue, has a revelation, has an interpretation. Let all things be done for edification." Here, "edification" is that of the church. While we may speak of edifying ourselves, the emphasis in the Bible is the edification of others. Whatever we do, or do not do, might have the effects of either building up, or stumbling, others in the faith. We have noted that when a person is converted, his world view changes from self in the centre of his thinking to having God at the centre. He then thinks of the edification of others, and finally the good of himself. We expect that one who grows to spiritual maturity will constantly think of glorifying God, edifying the church, and the good of self in that order of importance.

The teaching ministry of the church is geared to the salvation of souls and the edification of the members. We are told in Ephesians 4:11-16,

> And He Himself gave some to be apostles, some prophets, some evangelists, and some pastors and teachers, for the equipping of the saints for the work of ministry, for the edifying of the body of Christ, till we all come to the unity of the faith and of the knowledge of the Son of God, to a perfect man, to the measure of the stature of the fullness of Christ; that we should no longer be children, tossed to

and fro and carried about with every wind of doctrine, by the trickery of men, in the cunning craftiness of deceitful plotting, but, speaking the truth in love, may grow up in all things into Him who is the head—Christ— from whom the whole body, joined and knit together by what every joint supplies, according to the effective working by which every part does its share, causes growth of the body for the edifying of itself in love.

The extraordinary offices of apostle, prophet and evangelist have been withdrawn since the completion of Scripture. The ordinary office of the pastor-teacher remains in the church. While the pastor labours in word and doctrine, the members of the church are to avail themselves of his teaching in order to benefit from it. Growth in knowledge will be accompanied by growth in grace (cf. 2 Pet. 3:18). As one puts the truth into practice, faith is being exercised (cf. Heb. 5:14). As we grow in spiritual maturity, we are used by the Lord in the building up of the church. The truth of Ephesians 4:16 will be seen as "...the whole body, joined and knit together by what every joint supplies, according to the effective working by which every part does its share, causes growth of the body for the edifying of itself in love."

7.7   The Sanctification Of The Church

Our seventh, and last, point is that the pursuit of spiritual growth is to be with the sanctification of the universal church in view. God has chosen for Himself a people from eternity, who are saved in time, by grace through faith in Jesus Christ. We are being sanctified by the Holy Spirit individually in order that the local church might be sanctified. This will, in turn, contribute to the sanctification of the universal church. This truth is taught in Ephesians 5:25-27,

Husbands, love your wives, just as Christ also loved the church and gave Himself for her, that He might sanctify and cleanse her with the washing of water by the word, that He might present her to Himself a glorious church, not having spot or wrinkle or any such thing, but that she should be holy and without blemish.

We are told, further, in verse 32, "This is a great mystery, but I speak concerning Christ and the church." This must be understood in the light of Ephesians 3:14-19,

> For this reason I bow my knees to the Father of our Lord Jesus Christ, from whom the whole family in heaven and earth is named, that He would grant you, according to the riches of His glory, to be strengthened with might through His Spirit in the inner man, that Christ may dwell in your hearts through faith; that you, being rooted and grounded in love, may be able to comprehend with all the saints what is the width and length and depth and height— to know the love of Christ which passes knowledge; that you may be filled with all the fullness of God.

The apostle Paul has a big picture of God's plan. In Ephesians 1:3-14, he shows how the triune God has chosen for Himself a people from eternity past, to the praise of His glory in eternity future. In Ephesians 3:14-19, he sees how the sanctification of the local church will lead to the sanctification of the universal church. In Ephesians 4:11-16, he sees how the ministry of the word will edify the local church. In Ephesians 5:25-27, he affirms that the sanctification of the local church will lead to the sanctification of the universal church.

While our individual life is short and plays only a minute role in the purposes of God, it is nevertheless within the scope of God's ultimate purpose of gathering together His people, in Christ. There will come a time when the Lord returns to judge the world, and to gather together His people in the new heavens and the new earth, in which righteousness dwells (cf. 2 Pet. 3:10). Then will come the marriage supper of the Lamb (cf. Rev. 19:9). Then will take place what is described in Revelation 21:1-4,

> Now I saw a new heaven and a new earth, for the first heaven and the first earth had passed away. Also there was no more sea. Then I, John, saw the holy city, New Jerusalem, coming down out of heaven from God, prepared as a bride adorned for her husband. And I heard a loud voice from heaven saying, "Behold, the tabernacle of God is with men, and He will dwell with them, and they shall be His people. God Himself will be with them and

be their God. And God will wipe away every tear from their eyes; there shall be no more death, nor sorrow, nor crying. There shall be no more pain, for the former things have passed away."

This constitute the Christian hope. Our spiritual growth is to be pursued with the sanctification of the universal church in view.

7.8 Conclusion

Our text, which is 2 Timothy 2:22, has been studied plainly, in context, and by comparison with related scriptures. The text consists of three main parts. The first part is negatively stated – viz. that we are to flee youthful lusts, consisting of pleasures, power, and possessions. The second part is stated positively, viz. that we are to pursue godliness, faith, and love. The third part is that fleeing youthful lusts and pursuing spiritual virtues are to be done in the company of like-minded believers, in the context of the local church. What this entails for the individual has been delineated in seven points that are linked together in progression. It begins with a personal choice to obey the gospel, to separate from the world, to separate from nominalism, to commit oneself to the local church, to avoid negative influences, to edify the church, and to keep in view the big picture of the sanctification of the universal church.

A fitting close to this series of studies is the exhortation given in Ephesians 5:1-7,

> Therefore be imitators of God as dear children. And walk in love, as Christ also has loved us and given Himself for us, an offering and a sacrifice to God for a sweet-smelling aroma. But fornication and all uncleanness or covetousness, let it not even be named among you, as is fitting for saints; neither filthiness, nor foolish talking, nor coarse jesting, which are not fitting, but rather giving of thanks. For this you know, that no fornicator, unclean person, nor covetous man, who is an idolater, has any inheritance in the kingdom of Christ and God. Let no one deceive you with empty words, for because of these things the wrath

of God comes upon the sons of disobedience. Therefore do not be partakers with them.

= THE END =